Come
L'appetito vien
mangiando!

BUON NATALE

ABOUT THE AUTHOR

As a former international supermodel, Maria Liberati never dreamed that she would go from being a fashion diva to a domestic diva. Ironically, while jet setting off to modeling assignments around the world, Maria became closer to the simplicity of life and food in the country setting of her family's vineyard in the mountains of central Italy. She began to experience the real tastes of food that she knew from her childhood.

Her passion with food began at the early age of 4, when she would accompany 'nonno' (grandfather) on his early morning Saturday trips to the Italian Market in Philadelphia to pick out all the fresh ingredients for the Sunday family meal.

Years later, Maria was spotted by international artist Sergio Terzi (known as Nerone) and was asked to sit for a portrait at his studio in the Emilio-Romagna region of Italy. While sitting for this portrait, the months lingered on and Maria found herself spending more and more time at Nerone's family farm nearby. During her time there, she studied the art of making the famed Parmigiana-Reggiano cheese. When the painting was finished, it was exhibited all throughout the world including the Metropolitan Museum of Art where the painting and the artist were honored at a special ceremony for the contributions of Italians to the World.

Maria began writing food articles and restaurant review columns. She was soon asked to conduct cooking programs while in Italy and then in the States. The rest, as they say, is history.

Also a successful businesswoman, Maria is VP of Liberati Investment Corporation—www.liberaticorporation.com—an investment corporation headed by Maria's brother, John Liberati. She divides her time between her office and residence in the USA and Italy.

Maria's cooking philosophy that she shares here with you, is to create recipes that simply transform the freshest ingredients without changing their essential flavors. For more tips on cooking, foods, style and decorating, visit: www.marialiberati.com.

THE BASIC ART *of* ITALIAN COOKING
BY
Maria Liberati

Art OF LIVING, PrimaMedia, Inc.

DEDICATION

This book is for my nonni (grandparents). I learned many things from them.
They always knew how to create special dishes from the simplest foods.

Art OF LIVING, PrimaMedia, Inc.

Published by Art of Living, PrimaMedia, Inc.

Library of Congress Control Number: 2005905279

ISBN-13: 978-1-92891-100-5
ISBN-10: 1-92891-100-5
Printed in the United States of America

www.MariaLiberati.com For information call: 1.800.581.9020

Credits: Editor: Maria DiDanieli; Contributing Editor: Joan Myers; Photography by: John Liberati;
Make-up by: Amber Alkins; Hair by: Trish Fecca; Styling, layout and cover design by: Tina Myers

A fine primer for budding Italian chefs. The endearing and informative stories that are woven into the cookbook provide a wonderful backdrop to the well explainedbasic recipies of Italian cuisine.

CHEF MICHAEL DEGEORGIO,
EXECUTIVE CHEF, IL CORTILE RESTRAUNT, NYC SPECIALY FOOD CONSULTANT

A memoir about living in Italy and the pleasures of Italian food that makes a perfect gift. But the recipies are so delicous, you'll want to try it first yourself.

CHEF TELL ERHARDT,
4 TIME CORDON BLEU WINNER, TV CHEF, COOKBOOK AUTHOR

If you want to get a sense of true authentic Italian food and the flavor of living in the mountains of the untouched regions of Italy, like Abruzzo, not only do I recomend you to take the trip, but also that you make Maria Liberati's "The Basic Art of Italian Cooking" part of your library.

JIM COLEMAN,
TV HOST OF PBS SERIES "FLAVORS OF AMERICA" AND EXECUTIVE CHEF OF COLEMAN RESTRAUNT AT NORMANDY FAMRS

What better way to combat the stress of these hectic times than a delicious meal with family and friends? This new book is filled with simple recipies for wonderful Italian food that nourishes both body and soul. It's a treasure that I turn to again and again.

PATRICIA A. FARRELL, PH.D.,
CLINICAL PSYCHOLOGIST, CONSULTANT, COMMENTATOR, AND AUTHOR OF
"HOW TO BE YOUR OWN THERAPIST"

TABLE OF CONTENTS

V

THE BASIC ART *of* ITALIAN COOKING
is as much a feast for the senses as it is for the stomach.

A passionate and heartwarming look at the recipes
that connect Maria from her past to her present.

Join Maria on a tour of Italy through her refreshingly
straightforward recipes.

Experience the fresh fruit macedonia from her family's vineyard.
Taste the minted pears and parmigiano antipasto.
Enjoy the portrait painted of Maria at the famed Italian
artist Nerone's studio in the Parma region.

"Italian Cooking is never just a recipe,
it is the basic art of creating something special
from something simple and fresh."

ACKNOWLEDGMENTS

I could never have written this book without help and/or inspiration from the following family members and friends:

My parents who taught me to appreciate all things Italian.

My grandparents: Nonno Giovanni, who began taking me on his trips to the Italian Market in Philadelphia when I was four years old. He taught me how to pick out all the freshest fruits and vegetables for Sunday dinner; and Nonna Maria who spent time preparing everything for our great big Sunday family meals.

My great-grandparents, especially Bis-nonno Antonio who was killed in front of our vineyard by Nazi soldiers during their occupation of his town, and my great-aunt Angelina who was a personal chef for some members of the Italian Royal Family. I never met either of them, but their memory has always inspired me to learn about my family and create the meals that have been a part of its history.

All of the chefs at the agriturismi (bed-and-breakfasts with farms) throughout Italy, some famous and some just well-known in their towns, for creating dishes that can only be described as magnifico! And for assisting me with creating some of my own masterpieces.

Award-winning European artist and writer Sergio Terzi, known as Nerone, for including the portrait that he painted of me in his most important exhibits throughout the world. The time spent at his villa and studio in Reggio-Emilia was truly an artistic inspiration for me. My portrait is something that I will always cherish.

Alfonso, for his love and support in the kitchen and for taking me all around Italy and Europe in my pursuit of great chefs, wonderful foods and cooking techniques.

My brother, John for being a great business partner and friend.

And all my family and friends throughout the world who, in some way, have inspired me to write this book.

A special thanks to Raya Haig for many years of inspiring my style.

INTRODUCTION

With my first cookbook, I wanted to combine some of the most memorable moments of my life in Italy with the thing that has become my passion: food. By sharing these recipes with you, I hope that preparing Italian meals will become a passion for you also, and that these stories that are so dear to my heart will make the recipes more meaningful for you.

I have had the pleasure of interviewing many world famous chefs for articles that I have written in the past. I have also had the opportunity to actually work with chefs in Italy, some famous and some not so well known. I have found that the one quality that makes a chef wonderful and attentive to every detail of the meal is their passion rather than how many awards they have won or how many degrees they hold. Passion is the key ingredient to any wonderful meal.

As an international model, I was fortunate to have the opportunity to live and work all around the world. When I pursued a degree in Foreign Languages at Temple University in Philadelphia, I had no idea where it would take me or what I would do with that knowledge. Learning languages, experiencing different cultures and enjoying various cuisine all came together into one big wonderful experience that will be of value to me for the rest of my life.

Each time I traveled to a country that was new to me, I would experience the foods of that country. I soon came to study Italian cooking more intensively, first at my family's vineyard, and then at some of the most wonderful bed-and-breakfasts throughout different regions of Italy. You see, there is really no such thing as Italian cooking, per se. Each region of Italy has its own style of cooking, and I set out to experience the best of as many regions as possible. I hope this book will give you a taste of what I have experienced while traveling throughout the wonderful country of Italy.

From my trips as a child to the Italian market with my grandfather where he taught me how to pick out the freshest and best ingredients, to my time spent at the Liberati vineyard in the mountains of central Italy, my love for food began at an early age and has developed into a true passion. I remember those early jaunts to the Italian market almost as if they were yesterday. We would then take these wonderful ingredients back to nonna, or grandma, and we would begin preparing those unforgettable Sunday dinners. I would also watch in wonder as nonno used the grapes we had just bought to make his wine, the same wine that our family produced at his vineyard.

I am fortunate enough to be able to continue to divide my time between visits to my family's vineyard in Italy and the USA where I still make those nostalgic early Sunday trips with my mom to the Italian market in Philadelphia.

I have written this book with simplicity in mind. You see, simplicity is one of the keys to a great Italian meal. In Italy, cooking is considered an art, it is the art of taking a few of the freshest ingredients and turning them into a masterpiece. This book will show you how to make unforgettable dishes with basic, simple, but fresh, carefully chosen ingredients just like chefs in Italy have been doing for centuries!

This book has a second purpose as well. While I was modeling in Italy, a very famous Italian painter named Nerone painted my portrait. He then exhibited the painting at many galleries throughout Europe and at the Metropolitan Museum of Art in New York City, as well as in other locations throughout the United States. When he was done with displaying my picture, he gave it to me as a present. However, the "catch" was that I had to go to his studio and pick it up! Nerone's studio happens to be located in a beautiful, but very rural, part of Reggio-Emilia in the north of Italy. So, after picking it up, we had to fit this gigantic painting in the back of my fiancé's tiny European car, get it back to his studio in Rome, and then have it transported to my home in the United States. Many interesting things, and recipes, happened along the way. The stories of Nerone's art and my quest to claim my painting will be included here in this book for you to share with me along with recipes that, like Nerone's work, reflect the creativity and art of the Italian culture and the Italian people.

As I have mentioned, I would also like to share other stories of my experiences in Italy as I take you through the various courses of a typical Italian meal. Why? Because, no Italian meal is ever eaten in silence! Conversations float over the food like the clouds across the heavens, nonstop and never without something interesting taking shape! So, I will add my own conversation to our meal together with the hope that I can entertain you with my real stories about life in Italy.

I hope you will enjoy cooking these foods and sharing in my stories. As we say before we begin every meal "Buon'apetito!"

Don't forget to visit my web site, www.marialiberati.com, for more recipes as well as ideas on entertaining, foods, and the art of living.

PREFACE

The Italian Meal

THE ITALIAN MEAL BASICALLY CONSISTS OF FIVE SEGMENTS.

The antipasti is the first part; these are appetizers. They are light but delicious foods designed to whet your hunger and prepare your palate for what is to come.

Next, comes the primi. The word primi means the "first things" or "the firsts." This course is usually a pasta dish or risotto, perhaps a soup. If pasta or risotto is served, the quantity is usually not overly generous, as this course is a lead-in for the main course.

The main entree is called secondi or "the seconds," for obvious reasons. This usually involves a meat or fish dish and is the course that best defines the meal. It is the masterpiece that is carried in by the cook, on her most beautiful tray, for everyone to "ooh" and "ahh" over. It is the climax of the meal.

With the secondi, one serves side dishes, or contorni. These are not just a few vegetables tossed together but can be a specialty in themselves. The contorni punctuate the main statement made by the secondi and, as such, should be given great care and time. Fresh ingredients are the heart of great contorni.

The dolci, or sweets, that are served as dessert should end the meal by leaving your guests with a feeling of being satisfied, not stuffed, and united with those who have shared the meal around the table.

And last, but certainly not least, the wine or vino! You can choose several wines to complement the various portions of your meal or just one, usually the venerable creation made from the grape of one of the uncles (zii) or grandfathers (nonni) that would take you and the other diners through all the courses. It is not within the scope of this book to get into a detailed description of wines, but I may suggest a flavor or two that I think perfectly enhances my recipes.

Throughout every Italian meal, one hears good, warm, involved, and passionate conversation. In fact, there are usually several conversations going on at the same time, each competing in volume and drama with the others. So, along with recipes, I am going to converse with you throughout this book, taking you to the places and people that helped inspire me to develop these recipes and share them with you!

QUOTES

"We should look for some one to eat and drink with before looking for something to eat and drink."
Epicurus, Greek Philosopher

"Good painting is like good cooking; it can be tasted but not explained."
Unknown author

"Cooking is like love; it should be entered into with abandon or not at all."
Harriet van Horne

PART ONE
Antipasti

Italian

PREPARATION

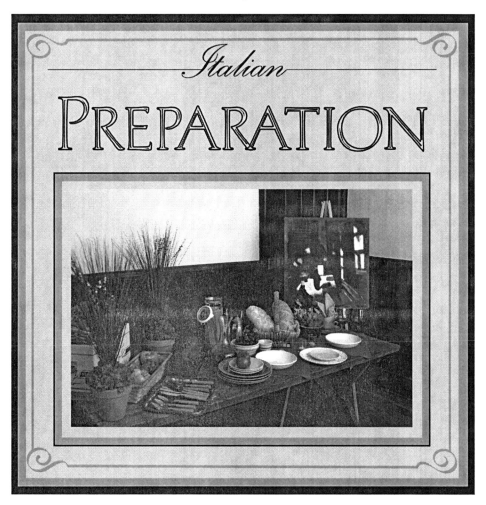

Most Italians include antipasti with special meals and not usually with an everyday meal. In the United States, we have huge antipasti plates with prosciutto (Italian ham), cheese, olives, vegetables, et cetera, that are presented for one person to eat. In Italy, one large plate is prepared and shared between a table of diners.

Bruschetta is perhaps the most popular type of antipasto and is served in many parts of the world outside of Italy, even in restaurants that do not typically serve Italian food.

Here are some bruschetta recipes along with other suggestions for antipasti that will get your stomach wishing for more!

Allow me tell you some stories while you enjoy your choice of antipasti.

CHAPTER 1

OLIVE OIL FIT FOR CAESAR

Recently, I visited a country farm that was once the summer home of Julius Caesar. It is easy to see why the Caesar family chose this spot, in the beguiling hills of Umbria, as their getaway. Our host at the farm graciously offered to take us on a tour of nearby Spillo, a medieval town known for its beauty. It is a citta d'arte, city of art, a designation awarded to few towns in Italy.

In a small Italian car, we wound up and down the streets of Spillo. Here the ambiance and beauty of Caesar's day lingers. The narrow streets are laid in small stone pieces called mosaics. The old center of town is built almost like one big villa divided into small apartments, which is exactly how it was used by the family of Julius Caesar.

We continued to climb in altitude until we reached the top of Spillo, a grand panorama that is simply called belvedere or "beautiful sight." (It is wise, when in Italy, to always pull over and stop at signs announcing belvedere; these parking spots offer a relaxing moment to reflect on the stunning landscape of Italy.)

It was a clear, sunny day so we could see much of pastoral Umbria and even, in the distance, Assisi and the famous church of St. Francis. The verdant hills and countryside rolled away at our feet, and I sighed as the peace of this ancient land seeped into my senses, perhaps in the same way it had offered respite to the busy Roman conqueror.

The Romans started the production of olive oil in Umbria, and there now exists a school dedicated to studying and perfecting the methods used in olive oil production. Some of the oldest olive plants in Italy are located here. No wonder some of the best olive oil in the world hails from Umbria.

And no wonder Umbria is famous for its bruschetta, what we call garlic bread. This popular appetizer gets its special taste from olive oil.

BRUSCHETTA

To make bruschetta, you must first get crusty Italian bread.

Bruschetta Gratinatta
1/4 pound fontina cheese
3 leaves of arugula
2 very ripe tomatoes
5 slices of crusty bread
1 tablespoon olive oil

Cut the fontina cheese into small slices.
Then, cut the tomatoes into very tiny cubes, eliminating the seeds.
Chop the arugula finely.

Put bread under broiler or on small grill till golden and crusty (approx. 2-5 minutes, oven times will vary). Remove from oven.

Drizzle half of the olive oil on bread slices. Sprinkle chopped arugula on top, then add tomatoes. Place cheese slices on top and place bruschetta in oven until cheese starts to melt and bubble. Put under broiler for 1-2 minutes to brown. Remove and serve immediately.

BRUSCHETTONE AL TONNO (BRUSCHETTA WITH TUNA)

1 can of tuna, preferably albacore or filet of tuna (with or without olive oil)
2 very ripe tomatoes
5 slices of large crusty bread
1 stalk of celery, chopped finely
fresh basil to taste, chopped finely
2 tablespoons extra virgin olive oil

Cut the tomatoes into small cubes, eliminating the seeds.
Put bread slices under broiler or on small grill till golden and crusty (approx 2-5 minutes, oven times will vary). Remove from oven.

If the tuna is in water, drain the water. If it is in olive oil, do not drain the olive oil.
Place, in a bowl, the tuna (flaked), tomato cubes, olive oil, celery and basil–toss this mixture lightly.

Place the mixture on top of each slice of bread and serve them individually.

CHAPTER 2

THE HOUSEWIFE STORE

All the small towns in Italy have a negozio per casalinghi (store for housewives) that carries supplies for the home, kitchen supplies, bath supplies, home decor items, and the increasingly popular electrical appliances (elettrodomestici).

But "store for housewives" is a term left over from antiquity. In the United States and in this age of political correctness, it would be unimaginable to shop at a store marketing itself to "housewives." Even the term "homemaker" has a 50's ring to it. In the diverse U.S. culture of two-income households, the one taking care of the home is not assumed to be a woman. A growing number of couples share household duties, making "househusbands" almost as common as "housewives."

But, in Italy, although things are slowly changing, the role of the housewife always has been, and is still thought to be, an important and unique one. So much so that the Italian government invented a special insurance for housewives. If a housewife is injured while cooking, cleaning, or taking care of her house, the insurance covers her. The government also has considered giving a special stipend to housewives, an hourly rate that housewives would get for staying at home.

As I wandered through a negozio per casalinghi, I pondered the Italian attitude toward women and their place in the home. Why do the Italian people just assume that everything domestic is done by a female? In addition to the housewives stores, there are arts-and-crafts books called "books for housewives." Do only women in Italy work in crafts for the home? It seemed to me, someone raised in an Italian American home, that Italy was a chauvinistic society. Even though I knew many men among my family and friends in Italy who cooked, women were still classified as the housewives.

While women are considered the housewives in Italy, in truth, they are also many other things: They hold important professional positions outside of the home; they work in the government; as lawyers, doctors, architects, judges, heads of companies, et cetera. However, Italian society, as a whole, still has what seems to be a somewhat antiquated way of thinking about females.

It offended me, initially, that everyone seemed to assume that I cooked just because I was female. When I would eat at my relatives' houses, there was always a female cousin whom, I was told, cooked well and that her cooking "kept her boyfriend or fiancé happy." And some of these female cousins who cooked were judges and lawyers, or studying to be one of these.

Once again, it sort of makes you think, is it offensive to assume that a female can cook well? I have come to the conclusion that it really is not and that our society has been attempting to be too politically correct over this issue. I love to cook in the Italian tradition because it is really an art, and I consider myself more of an artist than someone who just throws ingredients together. Italian society places an important emphasis on females being able to cook and take care of their house, but many men also cook in Italy, and they cook well!

For the Italian men, it is important to have a good meal waiting for them at lunchtime. It is something they expect. They have been spoiled by years of attention from their doting mothers and grandmothers. By "a good meal," I do not mean a grilled cheese sandwich and potato chips. Most Italian women will have a meal prepared for the men in their lives that would do any chef proud, even women who are accomplished professionals in their own work lives. They do this because they love to cook and because preparing a wonderful meal is considered an act of love, akin to giving a present.

FOCACCIA BREAD

The dough:
2¼ cups tepid water
2 teaspoons active dry yeast
¼ cup olive oil
6½ cups unbleached all purpose flour

These ingredients are to garnish the bread to taste:
olive oil
rosemary
grated cheese
salt

Mix ½ cup water and yeast together in a bowl.
This mixture will start to bubble together-when it does this, you know the yeast is working.
Combine flour and salt together in a large bowl.
Add the yeast mixture, the oil and 1¾ cup of water.
Blend the mixture and, if it is too stiff, add more water a little at a time. You want soft, sticky dough.

Place the dough on a floured board and knead it for about 10 minutes.
Then, place the dough in a greased bowl-cover it and allow it to rise for about 1 to 1½ hours until it doubles in size.
Punch it down with your fists and let it rise a second time.
Divide the dough into three equal pieces and shape each piece into a ball.
Place each ball into an oiled plastic bag and refrigerate for 24 hours.

Remove the dough from the refrigerator about 1½ hours before you are ready to work with it.
Place the dough on a floured board.
Cover it and let it come up to room temperature.
The dough should be doubled in size and should be spongy to the touch.

Heat the oven to 450 degrees F.
Place the dough on flat pans, brush it with olive oil, and sprinkle rosemary and/or grated cheese on top as well as salt to taste. Bake for 15-20 minutes or until golden.

Place the baked foccacia on a rack to cool.

STUFFED TOMATOES WITH BASIL

1 cup breadcrumbs
1 8-ounce can tuna packed in olive oil
1 tablespoon capers
6 small, round, firm tomatoes
1 lemon
fresh Italian parsley
fresh basil

Cut the off tops of the tomatoes and save these tops for later.
Gently remove the seeds and pulp.
Sprinkle a pinch of salt over each of the tomatoes to dry out slightly.
Then, place the tomatoes upside down on absorbent paper towel and let them dry out for about 30 minutes.
Place, in a bowl, the breadcrumbs with tuna and the olive oil.
Mix thoroughly by hand.
Then, add a handful of chopped parsley and the capers with the grated peel of one lemon.
Mix by hand again.
Then, add the juice of one lemon.
Filter the seeds and pulp from the juice.
Mix all ingredients again, by hand, until they are well blended.

Divide the mixture evenly and place some in each tomato.
Place the tops back on the tomatoes and garnish with fresh basil leaves.
You can also drizzle a little olive oil on top when serving.

CHAPTER 3

BELLEZZA ITALIANA

In Italy, everything must be bellezza or "beautiful." The presentation of Italian food is just as important as the quality of the food. This doesn't mean you have to polish the silver serving pieces for every meal, but it does mean taking the time to present the meal and your dishes with a flourish. Personally, I love to serve my Italian meals on an attractive tray; it just makes everything seem a little more special.

Striving for beauty, in everything from the food you are serving to the clothes you are wearing, is part of everyday life in Italy. At home in the U.S., I throw on my gym workout clothes and a big pair of sunglasses and go to the supermarket. Why do my hair or makeup just to select peppers in the vegetable aisle? Such inattention to appearance would elicit a gasp of shock from an Italian woman. In Italy, even a pair of jeans is paired with a tasteful shirt or sweater and an elegant scarf to match. You must add a little touch that makes people think of your outfit as beautiful. Sometimes it is tiring because just to go around the corner to the fruit market, or to the "housewife store," or to the neighborhood coffee bar, you must go dressed sharply.

The only people who seem exempt from this unspoken rule are the older, gray-haired women, mainly grandmothers, who live in the very small Italian towns. One beautiful, sunny Sunday morning, in search of a good gelato place, we drove through two such towns. Saint Giovanni and Saint Maria are located next to each other. Their piazzas are made up of a little circle in front of the town church. There we found a small coffee bar, a bread/pizza bakery, a dolci bakery, and a grocery/housewife store. (These towns were too small to have separate stores for groceries and "housewife" supplies, so they were combined into one.)

When you drive through such towns as Saint Giovanni and Saint Maria, especially before lunch on a Sunday, you are guaranteed a view of the local grandmothers walking to the grocery store wearing a housecoat and slippers. Some of them may actually still have their hair in curlers. In the winter, they will simply throw a coat over their housecoat. While growing up, I used to see the older Italian women in Philadelphia and Little Italy go to the local market the very same way. These women venture out to get the ingredients for their afternoon meal. When the meal is almost ready to eat, they will then take the time to remove their curlers, exchange their housecoat for a dress, and do their makeup and hair. Their makeup will be light (since Italian women generally are blessed with good complexions) and their jewelry not overly done. They will be beautiful, just as the meal they are serving is.

DEVIL'S ANTIPASTO OR ANTIPASTO AL DIAVALO

8 slices of thinly sliced white bread
2 red peppers
1 yellow pepper
1 cup tomato paste
10 basil leaves
1 garlic clove
2 tablespoons pinoli (pine) nuts
extra virgin olive oil
salt
cayenne pepper

Clean the peppers and cut them into small cubes.

Place 3 tblsps. olive oil in and garlic in saüt pan and heat. When oil just starts to bubble,
add in peppers, then tomato paste.
Add salt and pepper to taste.
Let this mixture simmer on low heat, covered, for 20 minutes.
At the end, place the washed and dried basil leaves in the mixture.
Remove from heat, cover, and let stand.

Remove crusts from the bread slices.
Cut each slice in two and brown each half in very hot oil-corn oil or sunflower seed oil-on both sides.
Place slices on an absorbent paper towel.
Place pinoli nuts in a small cup with a spoonful of olive oil and let them absorb the oil.
Then, spread the vegetable mixture on the bread slices while they are still warm.
Garnish the slices with the pinoli nut in oil.

CROSTINI NAPOLETANA

4 thick slices of bread (crusty Italian type)
2 ounces of fresh mozzarella cheese
2 ounces tomato paste
8 anchovy fillets
olive oil
oregano
salt and pepper to taste

Using an oil can that has a thin spout, pour a light coating of olive oil on each slice of bread
Then equally divide the tomato paste among the 4 slices of bread.
Place 2 anchovy fillets on each slice of bread.
Sprinkle with oregano and then add salt and pepper.
Slice mozzarella cheese and place on top of bread.
Place baking paper on a baking pan and coat it lightly with oil.
Place each slice of bread on the baking paper
Then bake for about 5 minutes at 400 degrees For until the cheese melts and becomes bubbly.

This recipe serves four people.

CORNETTI DI PROSCIUTTO CON NOCE
(HAM CONES WITH NUTS)

4 slices of prosciutto ham
4 ounces of cream cheese
3 ounces of shelled walnuts
a handful of parsley leaves

Set aside 4 whole walnuts and grind, or finely chop, the rest.
Place the cream cheese in a bowl and, with a wooden spoon, mix in the ground nuts.
Mix well.
Add about 1 teaspoon of finely chopped parsley leaves.
Mix well.

Divide the mixture between 4 slices of prosciutto ham and spread the mixture onto each slice.
Shape each slice of prosciutto into a cone, or horn.
At the opening of each horn, place a whole walnut.
Place all four slices on a serving plate and garnish with parsley leaves.

Ingredients

PASTA, FLOUR, GARLIC

CHAPTER 4

A SPECIAL DAY

It's Sunday. The church bells are ringing, and I am joining everyone else in a stroll, or a passeggiata, in the piazza. The idea is to be noticed. But strutting like a peacock is not the only purpose of the Sunday morning passeggiata. It is also important to socialize, to stop before lunchtime at a local coffee bar for an espresso and pastry, then a snack at 11 a.m. or noon to hold one over until lunch is served at 2 p.m., and to shop for pasta.

The Sunday morning passeggiata almost always includes a trip to the pasta store. Pranzo (lunch) on Sundays usually is a special meal, and, in Italy, fresh pasta is mandatory for special meals. For meals on holidays, such as Christmas, Easter, the Epiphany, or New Years, fresh pasta is made at home. When you buy fresh pasta, if it is made by a talented pasta maker, it is almost as good as homemade. I say almost as good because the only ingredient missing is the "love" mixed into the pasta, along with the flour, by your mother, nonna or zia (aunt).

Local pasta stores carry an assortment of pasta, therefore, you can buy fresh ravioli to complement the sugo (sauce) or fresh tagliatelle to make with the tartufi (truffles). If you want a specific type of pasta to accompany a special ingredient or sauce you have made, just ask the expert pasta maker to recommend the pasta and its thickness.

Lasagna, which is always served on holidays, has to be made with fresh pasta layers. No self-respecting Italian would dare to not serve a lasagna to family and friends for a special meal. So, if you do not have the time or the energy to make the fresh pasta, cheat and buy it. Lasagna made with fresh pasta and fresh mozzarella is an experience for the palate that is worth the time and hard work involved in its preparation.

Of course, after the pasta store, we continue on our passeggiata to the forno. The aroma of bread, just plucked from the oven, guides us there. Even though bread is not eaten directly with pasta, it is important to have a fresh loaf on hand. Bread is usually served before or after the pasta course with the salad, as a second course, or as an appetizer.

LASAGNA VERDE BOLOGNESE STYLE

For the sauce:
½ onion chopped finely
1 carrot chopped finely
1 stalk of celery chopped finely
2 tablespoons butter
½ pound ground beef
1/3 pound ground pork
¼ pound ground veal
1 cup of tomato sauce
salt and pepper to taste

For the lasagna:
1 pound white flour
2 eggs
½ pound spinach
béchamel sauce (recipe in Part IV)
Butter
Grated Parmigiana-reggiano cheese

Fry the vegetables in butter, add the meat, and brown for a few minutes.
Then add the plain tomato sauce, salt and pepper to taste.
Prepare the pasta by mixing the flour, eggs, and spinach.
(The spinach should be freshly cooked, dried, and passed through a potato masher or food processor.)
Mix all ingredients and roll the dough out on a floured board.
Cut the dough into large rectangular squares, dust with semolina flour, and let it stand.

Butter a large lasagna pan. On the bottom, put a small amount of sauce and grated cheese
Then top this with a layer of lasagna.
Cover this layer of lasagna with more sauce, cheese, and, also, béchamel sauce
Then repeat with another layer of lasagna.
The final layer should be topped with bechamel sauce and a pat of butter.

Bake the lasagna in the oven at 320 degress F for approximately 30 minutes or until the top becomes slightly golden.

For a variation, this can be made without the meat and just with vegetables.

RISOTTO PARMIGIANA

400 grams carnaroli or Arborio rice
1 small onion chopped finely
4 ounces Parmigiana-reggiano cheese, grated
1 tblsp. Butter
4 tablespoons extra virgin olive oil
1 cup broth-chicken or vegetable
1 glass dry white wine
Salt to taste

In a large frying pan, combine the olive oil and broth.
Sauté the onion in this mixture.
When the onion is golden, add the rice and allow it to become a golden color.
Add the white wine a little at a time and the broth a little at a time.
Stir, all the while keeping the stove on low heat. You should cook the mixture for 15 minutes.
When the rice is al dente, add the rest of the butter and half of the grated cheese, stir gently.
Continue to stir.

Place in individual serving dishes and sprinkle with the remaining cheese. Serve hot.

CHAPTER 5
PICNIC AL FRESCO

It was the dead of August, and everyone was either at the beach or in the mountains enjoying their summer vacation. On this quiet summer day, the view from my patio called to me: The mountains were irresistible, the church steeple was picturesque, and my own garden reminded me of the glorious meals we had enjoyed and those that still awaited us. The artichokes were just finished, but the organic rosemary and mint were ready. There were trees that bore susine (small plums), pears, and hazelnuts. It was the perfect setting for a picnic.

So I began planning a meal that we could eat outside, or al fresco. When Italians eat, the food and the presentation are important. So I planned not only the menu of insalata di riso, fagioli con prezzemolo, and fragole con limone, but also how I would serve them. I would need an attractive vassoio (tray) large enough to hold all the serving dishes. The wine, mineral water, glasses, silverware, and dishes could be carried out to the patio without a tray, but not my mouth-watering food. I chose a bright tablecloth for the picnic table. Although I considered the traditional picnic utensils and china, plastic silverware and paper dishes, the truth is Italian food and plastic silverware, or paper dishes, just do not go well together. It would be like placing a work of art on a piece of cardboard instead of a canvas.

Insalsata di riso is a popular dish for the summertime. It is light, refreshing, and easy to transport in containers to the beach, or wherever you are having a picnic. This salad is extremely adaptable, it works well with vegetables fresh from your summer garden as well as leftovers from your fridge. (Although leftovers are almost a no-no here in Italy, they are usually given to the stray cats and dogs that wander the streets.) But if you have some chicken or vegetables that are left over from dinner, place them in the refrigerator, and, the following day, slice or chop them to mix them into the salad.

My favorite rice salad is made with tuna canned in extra virgin olive oil or with fresh shrimp. (Frozen shrimp just won't do.) Fresh celery; luscious tomatoes; cooked peas and string beans; green or black olives; your preferred beans-ceci (chick peas) or cannellini beans, all fresh, soaked the night before, and cooked; fresh mozzarella cheese balls; or small chunks of fresh mozzarella, provolone, or Emmenthal cheese, all make good additions to a flavorful tuna and rice salad.

INSALATA DI RISO (RICE SALAD)

Prepare this recipe at least two hours before eating so that all the flavors have a chance to soak in.

1 cup dried rice
1 can, 6-8 ounces, of tuna (albacore) packed in extra virgin olive oil
1 cup cherry tomatoes
½ pound fresh mozzarella cheese
2 stalks of celery with leaves
½ cup ceci beans (chick peas)
(if dry, soak overnight and then cook until tender; cool the ceci beans before adding them to the salad)
2 tablespoons extra virgin, cold pressed olive oil

Use a good rice, preferably not instant, and cook it according to the instructions on the package. Drain the rice and let it cool.

Flake the tuna in a small dish.
Cut the mozzarella cheese into small chunks; not too small because fresh mozzarella will break easily. (Alternately, you can use cilegini mozzarella balls-you don't need to cut these.)

Wash and cut the celery stalks into slices-not too thin-and be sure to pull off any threads from the celery. Chop celery leaves finely.

Place cooled rice in a large bowl with all the other ingredients, drizzle olive oil on top of the salad, Gently mix.

Add salt to taste. Save some celery leaves to garnish the top of the salad.

Once the ingredients are mixed, cover and refrigerate them for two hours.

CHAPTER 6

UN'IDEA ECCELLENTE

It was an unexpected trip.

It began with Alfonso's voglio, or desire, to ride a fast train and my voglio for some great Tuscan food and ideas for my Tuscan bean soup recipe. That is how we ended up in a field of sunflowers near a beautiful agriturismo, or bed-and-breakfast, in the Tuscan hills.

As Italians, we are impulsive, but it is not always easy for me to give into this impulsiveness. It still seems strange to me to wake up one morning in our studio in Rome and decide to hop a train to Florence.

In the United States, if I need to go into Manhattan or Philadelphia, I plan the trip at least twenty-four hours in advance. If I am going farther than that, say, to a destination that is more than an hour away, my arrangements may take a week to make. I leave nothing, not my hotel, route, or itinerary, to chance. But in Italy, I am learning to follow the expression, "When in Rome, do as the Romans do." I am learning to be spontaneous.

So, that day we followed our voglio to see Firenze, or Florence. (By the way, in Italy, one cannot just say one feels like having a meal. Instead, the dramatic Italians have a voglio for a meal. You can even use the word to mean you love someone or that you have a desire for someone. One quickly learns that every-thing, even the simple task of sitting down to lunch-is an opera here.)

In our quest to follow our voglio, we made our way to the train station. We did not know the departure or arrival time of the high-speed pentolino, which is reputed to get you from Rome to Florence in about one hour and thirty minutes instead of the usual two hour travel time.

It was a beautiful, sunny day in Rome, not that sun is anything out of the ordinary here. Rome is always favored with sun. It was an excellent day to travel, and everyone else seemed to have the same idea. The line at the train station was long and slow with people buying tickets and asking questions. They were ask-ing questions because, probably like us, they had just risen that morning and, without any planning, had also decided to go somewhere.

The crowd grew restless and angry. Many travelers had to get their tickets before their trains left, and so, several were shouting for service at one poor man behind the ticket counter. Alfonso edged closer to the counter to investigate why it was taking so long. He discovered that while one man worked furiously to provide tickets to the anxious mob of about fifty people, two of his coworkers, who were supposed to be helping with ticket sales were sitting in front of a television set behind the counter watching a soccer match. (Rome was in the playoffs for the national championships, which they eventually won that year.) It was obvious that to these men, cheering (or jeering, as the case may be) the home team was more important than helping passengers catch their trains.

While Alfonso wrestled to the front of the line, I tracked down a schedule, and, if it was correct, the only pentolino of the day would be leaving in about twenty-five minutes. We had to quickly get our tickets and be on our way! I shouted to Alfonso to "Hurry!" (sbrigati!)

The line was not moving, so we took matters into our own hands and asked for the manager. Unfortunately, the manager was one of the two guys watching the soccer match, and needless to say, he was not particularly sympathetic to our plight.

A fresh uproar began when some of the other people in line noticed that there were more workers at the train station, just sitting around and watching TV! (Italians usually do have loud discussions about everything from politics to waiting in line to talking about their favorite soccer match. It is a normal thing, and once the discussion is over, they wish each other a good day and are on their way.)

Finally, because the chaos was interfering with their soccer game watching, no doubt, the manager ordered a woman worker from the back to work the counter. She was obviously on unfamiliar ground, and was not well informed about the schedule, but she persevered and got the job done. We all got our tickets and found out that we needed to go to binario otto, or track eight, to get our train. As we climbed onto the train, it pulled away. We had just made it!

This is usually the scenario here, in Italy. Somehow or other, the job always gets done. Italians have, it seems, almost no method, yet they always get things done in their own creative way. I think this creativity is nurtured in the people of Italy from when they are young. And it is a creativity that often makes its way into their cooking.

ZUPPA DI LENTICCHIE (LENTIL SOUP)

2 cups dried lentils
3-4 tablespoons olive oil
2 garlic cloves
2 slices of onions
3-4 cups vegetable broth
2 carrots, sliced (optional)
2 potatoes (optional)
1 stick celery, sliced

Soak the lentils in a large bowl of water the night before-or at least 8 hours before-cooking this recipe.

Place oil with garlic cloves and onion slices in a deep saucepan or a large pot.
Heat just until the onions start to become golden.

Pre-cook the potatoes for 3-5 minutes in a pot of boiling water.

In a saucepan, mix lentils with some broth, potatoes, carrots, and celery.
Add more broth as needed.
When the lentils are tender, the soup is done; approximately 20-30 minutes.

Serve hot with home made crostini, or croutons (see Part IV).

ITALIAN WEDDING SOUP OR STRACCIATELLA SOUP BROTH

1 pound stewing chickens, chicken wings, backs, necks
1 medium onion
4 stalks celery with leaves
1 medium-sized carrot
1 medium-sized turnip
1 medium-sized rutabaga
2 anise bulbs
1 medium-sized parsnip
8 sprigs Italian parsley
½ teaspoon salt

THE BROTH
Wash the chicken in salt water and then rinse it with clear water.
Add 3 quarts of water to a large stockpot.
Add the chicken and vegetables to the water and bring it to a boil.
Reduce heat and simmer for about 2½ hours.
Skim off the foam that rises to the surface.
Place a colander over a large bowl and strain the stock through the colander.

THE SOUP
Cook escarole in broth for approx 10 minutes or till tender. Add in the meatballs and simmer for 5 minutes more.
Crostini or croutons for soup

Boil the escarole until tender and, then drain it, cut it, and place in the broth.
Cook broth with escarole for 10 minutes or to taste.
Add the meatballs and simmer a while longer.

Place the soup in soup bowls and place some croutons on top.

The recipe for "Crostini per zuppa," or croutons for soup, can be found in Part IV of this book.

LINGUINE ALLE VONGOLE

1 pound linguine
4 tablespoons olive oil
3-4 cloves garlic
1 pound fresh steamed clams
1 tablespoon parsley
½ lemon (to squeeze over pasta when finished)

Begin boiling water for the pasta before making the clam sauce.

Sauté crushed or whole garlic in a pan until it starts to become golden-about three minutes.
Add the clams and sauté for 5 minutes, add chopped parsley and sauté for about one minute.
Remove from fire.

Boil water for the pasta in a large, tall pasta pot.
Put the linguine in the boiling water
Follow the cooking directions on the side of the package for al dente pasta.
Drain the pasta and place it in the pan to sauté with the clam sauce.
Turn gently with a "pasta pincer" until the pasta is coated with sauce.
Squeeze the ½ lemon over the pasta and turn gently to coat the pasta.
Sprinkle fresh parsley on top.
Serve.

CHAPTER 7

VEDUTA DI FIRENZE

The comfortable, high-speed pentolino pulled into Florence in exactly one hour and thirty minutes, as advertised. We had sped through the Italian countryside to arrive at a city that begged to be taken at a leisurely pace. With its people and food, Florence is quite different from Rome.

Florence has such an elegant, sophisticated feel. Rome can be sophisticated as well, but the people there can generally be quite blunt, no sugarcoating! Ask a local shopkeeper in Rome for directions and you may get a sarcastic "What do I know?" In Florence, if they do not know where something is, they are likely to quietly tell you they do not know or direct you to someone who can tell you. Florentines just tend to be a quieter people.

Perhaps, it is because Florence, with its world-renown art and stunning architecture, invites one to pause in reflection. When we got off the train, we did not hurry to get settled in at the agriturismo. Instead, we headed to the Piazza De La Signoria, where the copy of the statue David stands. It is the main piazza in Florence. The city hall, known as the Palazzo Vecchio, is there as well. Nearby is an elegant coffee bar, and, since it was mid-morning, we decided an espresso and a small pastry were in order. Even though a cup of espresso is just a small quantity of coffee, it provides the jolt of energy one needs to explore the many sights of Florence.

We began our tour by wandering through the Uffizi Gallery, home to some of the most glorious artwork in the world. Here are sculptures by Michelangelo Buonaroti, Galileo Galilei, Amerigo Vespucci, and others who had enjoyed the patronage of wealthy Florentine families.

If you are in Florence and pressed for time, the best place to see an overview of the city is the Piazzale Michelangelo, which is named after one of Florence's most famous residents. This piazza sits up high and you can take in the splendid view of the Chiesa di Sante Croce, the beautiful Ponte Vecchio, Santa Maria del Fiore, and, to its right, Giotto's Tower and the tower of one of Florence's first great basilicas, Santa Maria Novella. Santa Maria Novella has a pharmacy that has been in operation since the seventeenth century. It is known for its high-quality body care preparations, which are marketed under the Santa Maria Novella brand and are popular with royalty and the upper crust of Europe.

RISOTTO CON CIPOLLE

1 cup Arborio rice
2 cups broth-vegetable or chicken
¼ cup white wine (optional)
½ sweet onion
olive oil
Grated parmigiano-reggiano cheese

Place 2-3 tablespoons of olive oil in a saucepan.
Dice or slice the onion.
When the oil has heated, place the onions into it and sauté them until they begin to become golden.

Add the rice with just enough broth to moisten it.
When the broth disappears, add more and continue doing this until the rice is cooked-about 15 minutes.
Then add the white wine.

When the risotto is done, place it in serving plates and top it with grated cheese.
You can also top it with 1 tablespoon of butter.

MINESTRA DI POMODORO (TOMATO SOUP)

1 cup extra virgin olive oil
3 cloves of garlic
handful of basil leaves, chopped
16 ounces tomato paste
1 slice of bread
salt and pepper to taste

Fry the garlic and chopped basil in olive oil.
Mix in the tomato paste.
Season with salt and pepper to taste.
Cook on medium heat for 20 minutes.

Add in the slice of bread and cover the bread with hot water.

Cover the soup and let it cook on low heat for about one hour.

Serve the soup when it is warm.

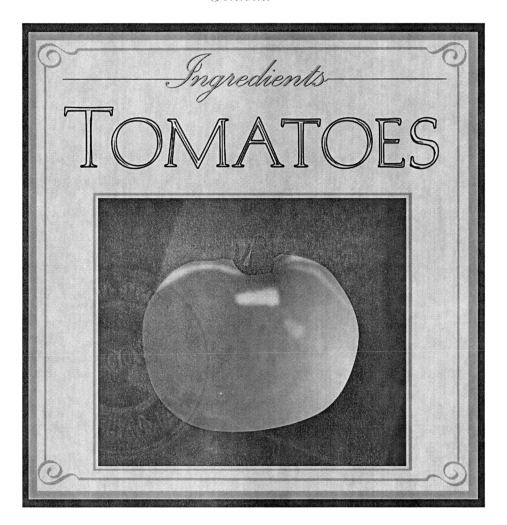

Ingredients

TOMATOES

CHAPTER 8
VIAGGIO IN AUTOBUS

The bus trip along the sides of the mountain from Sorrento to Amalfi will have you on the edge of your seat. The narrow road twists and turns as it grips the edge of the mountain. It is a daring road, which sometimes does not even supply guardrails. The Italian bus drivers seem to be accustomed to those conditions and are not upset by them in the least. When one bus is going down and another bus is coming up the mountain, one bus simply stops and pulls to the side so the other can pass. The drivers wave at each other, and we are all on our merry way, until the buses meet again.

We experienced this gut-clenching bus ride on the way to visit my cousin who lives in Positano. When we arrived in Positano, the bus took us to the center of the town. That is where we met my cousin and spent a lovely day walking, catching up on family news, and absorbing the quiet beauty of small Positano. It was mid-June, so of course, everyone was on the beach. We decided to catch the late-afternoon bus home. We were not eager to make the trip down the mountain in the dark. We doubted the roadway would be well lit.

We walked to the place where a bus should arrive momentarily and waited. A half an hour passed and still there was no bus. We had been told, originally, that the buses came by in the day at every hour on the hour. We asked a local gentleman walking by if he knew what time the bus was scheduled to arrive.

"Well," he said, "yesterday it came at 4:00, but I don't know what time it will come today."

"Doesn't the bus come at the same time every day?" I asked.

"Dipende," he answered. Dipende means "that depends." On what, I hadn't a clue.

At 5 p.m., before the dark set in, a bus arrived. We traveled back to Sorrento, again gripping the edges of our seats.

While transportation in Italy can be iffy, the food of this land is anything but. Even contorni, the side dishes, are prepared with precision, care, and fresh ingredients. The main course depends on a bold contorni to provide the perfect complement.

PURE DI PATATE

1¼ pound potatoes
3 tablespoons butter (left at room temperature)
4 tablespoons grated Parmigiana cheese
1 egg
2¼ cups milk
salt to taste
nutmeg (if you like)

Wash the potatoes well and place them in lightly salted cold water.
(The salt will prevent the skin of the potato from breaking during cooking.)
Be sure the potatoes are totally submerged in the water.
Once the water starts to boil, allow the potatoes to cook for 20 minutes.

Drain the potatoes and remove the peel.
Mash the potatoes in the potato masher while they are still hot.
Cut the butter into small pieces and add it to the mashed potatoes.
Add the grated cheese and a pinch of salt.
Heat the milk to a boil and add it to the potato mixture also.
Beat the potatoes with an electric hand-held beater, on slow speed, until the mixture is light and fluffy.

Serve immediately.

PATATE BELLE AL FORNO (OVEN-BAKED DECORATED POTATOES)

½ cup extra virgin olive oil
1 teaspoon salt
4 sprigs of rosemary
4 sprigs parsley
4 russet baking potatoes

Preheat the oven to 425 degrees F.

Pour half of the olive oil onto the bottom of a baking pan or glass baking dish.
Wash the potatoes and cut them in half, horizontally.
Press a rosemary sprig and the parsley into the four halves of the potatoes on the cut side.
Place the potatoes cut side down on the oil in the pan.
Drizzle tops of potatoes with more olive oil.
Bake for approximately 40-45 minutes until potatoes are nice and golden-browned and crispy.

You may want to broil them for 5 minutes at the end to make them brown and crispy.

Remove the potatoes from the oven. Place the potatoes on a serving dish, cut side up.

PATATE PER FESTE (HOLIDAY POTATOES)

1 pound potatoes
1 small onion
salt to taste
2 tablespoons butter

Place the potatoes in a large saucepan and add water over them until they are covered with water.
Add in a pinch of gross salt.
Boil the potatoes until they are tender.
Drain and cool the potatoes.

Mash the potatoes.
Finely chop the onions and add them to the potatoes.
Season with salt to taste, add butter and mix.
Place the mixture into small muffin cups.
Place some rosemary or parsley on top.

Bake at 425 degrees F for 35-40 minutes.
Remove the potatoes from the muffin cups and serve.

CHAPTER 9

AMORE, ITALIAN STYLE

When my hair stylist got married and moved to her husband's town to open a salon there, I put off finding her replacement as long as possible. It is difficult to trust one's hair to a stranger. My former stylist had been well known, having provided salon services for the Miss Italia contestants as well as some of the sfilate, or fashion shows, in Rome. I did not relish having to break in a new stylist.

Eventually, my hair became too frightening for even me to look at, so I took the plunge and walked into a salon located near Alfonso's studio. It is run by Solide and Katia, two sisters in their early thirties. Immediately, I saw that this was a gossipy type of salon, one of those small, intimate settings where local women let down their hair, literally and figuratively. While women sat through the rigors of a color or perm, they had plenty of time to share the latest news on who was getting married or divorced, who was having a baby or an affair, and other colorful goings-on.

Even to someone only slightly familiar with the Italian language, it is easy to make out the words suocera (mother-in-law) and cognata (daughter-in-law) in such conversations. Somebody always has something to vent about their mother-in-law or daughter-in-law in Italy.

Upon arriving, I asked per un appuntamento, that is, for an appointment. I was told to have a seat and that a stylist would be with me shortly. Since I was not in a rush–I just wanted to be sure that I got out in time to go to the mercato, the market, which closes at 1 p.m.; I had to buy fresh vegetables to make the minestra, or soup, for lunch–I decided to sit and wait.

In front of me, there were two chairs set next to each other. While Solide and Katia worked, their clients carried on an interesting repartee.

Today's topic of discussion seemed to be about Franco. (I was already aware of this story as news travels fast in the piazza.) Apparently, Franco had two families, a wife and grown children here in his native Italy and another wife and more children in Canada where he spent much of his time working.

Franco, a man now in his sixties, was a contractor who had decided to seek his fame and fortune in Canada. He obtained several lucrative contracts for local schools. As his business grew, Franco was regularly called upon to maintain the school buildings during the school year. This required that he spend more time in Canada. It seemed Franco had everything going for himself in Canada, except a wife and kids. He already had a set of them back home in Italy, but why transport them? So, Franco took himself a Canadian wife, bought a house, and eventually, had two children with his new wife. He still shares a house with them, in Canada, during the school year when he is needed for work there. In the summer and during Christmas holidays, Franco comes back to be with his wife and kids here in Italy.

The topic of the gossip at the hair salon today, besides what Franco was doing, was that his Italian family knew about their Canadian counterparts, but refused to acknowledge the situation! If you talked to one of his children, they were all married now, they would mention Dad and how he is off in Canada, but just ignore the fact that Dad had another wife and family there.

Although, to someone like me who was raised in a monogamous society, this seems indecent and hardly fair to either wife, such convenient arrangements are common in Italian culture. Thirty or fifty years ago, Italian men left their wives and children behind to go to the United States in search of work. While in America, they would sometimes take an American wife, have children, and then maybe return to Italy every few years to see their Italian family. Surprisingly, they continued to faithfully send support money to their wives in Italy.

As I sat in the salon, listening to the amorous adventures of Franco, I was reminded that Italians never live life half-heartedly. Even their food, including supporting characters like the contorni, must perform with passion.

FAGIOLI CON PREZZEMELO

1 pound fresh string beans
2 tablespoons olive oil
3 fresh cloves of garlic
1/3 cup freshly chopped parsley

Take the tips off the ends of the string beans.
Cook the beans until they are al dente or steam them leaving the tenderness to your liking. (Do not make them too mushy, or you will lose all the flavor and vitamins.)
Once the beans are cooked, drain them and let them cool to room temperature.

Chop the fresh garlic and parsley.
Place the beans in a small bowl, put in the garlic and parsley, and gently stir.
Drizzle olive oil on top and let the beans stand for about 20 minutes so that the flavors have time to soak in.

This dish can be served cold so you can refrigerate it before you serve it. It also makes a great picnic food, as well.

FINOCCHIO E PISELLI (FENNEL AND PEAS)

1 pound fresh or frozen sweet peas
1 stalk fresh anise (finocchio) chopped
¼ cup butter
salt to taste

In a saucepan, bring water to a boil with a pinch of salt in it.
When the water is boiling, add in the peas and chopped anise.
Cook for 10 minutes and drain.

Place the peas and anise in a serving dish, add butter, and let it melt on the vegetables.

Serve.

SPINACI FIORENTINA

2 pounds fresh spinach
4 eggs
4 ounces butter
2½ cups milk
Grated Parmigiana cheese
Flour salt and pepper to taste

Clean the spinach and cook it for about 10 minutes.
Drain it and remove all the water.
Chop it finely and place it in a casserole with half of the butter and a little salt.

In another pan, prepare a béchamel sauce-see Part IV in this book,
For the béchamel recipe-with the rest of the butter, milk, and 2 tablespoons of grated cheese.

Place the spinach in a glass pan that has been buttered.
With a small spoon, make 4 small holes in the spinach in the pan and, in each hole, place a whole egg.
Salt and pepper the egg and cover it with the béchamel sauce.
Place the grated cheese on top and bake in the oven at 360 degrees F for about 20 minutes.

HISTORICAL NOTE:

For some strange reason, all dishes described as "Fiorentina" have a base of spinach, and because of the influence of the French cooks who were employed by the noble families in Florence, many of the spinach dishes include béchamel sauce.

CHAPTER 10
AT MY GRANDFATHER'S VINEYARD

Tagliacozzo is the small town, as we say, "piccolo paese," where my grandfather was born. In the 1950s and 1960s, it was the summer and winter playground for people from Rome. Located in the mountains, it was cool in the summertime and perfect for mountain climbing and horseback riding. In the winter, Italian movie stars came here to ski. Tagliacozzo was less expensive and quieter than places like Cortina D'Ampezzo and Porto Cervo. However, once it became popular, prices began rising and the cost of hotel rooms and food rose to equal that of the traditionally more expensive resorts. Soon, the tourists stopped coming, and now the town retains a certain quiet charm. Although some areas, such as the old center of town, are badly in need of restoration, there are also some beautiful historical churches in Tagliacozzo including a church with cloistered nuns.

And it is here where my family planted their roots alongside the grape vines. My grandfather, or nonno, was one of thirteen brothers and sisters. Ziei Pietro and Mario (my uncles) and Zia Annina (my aunt) were the closest in age to him and the only relatives, along with their children, who are still surviving.

I arrived for my first visit to Tagliacozzo by train. As I got off the train, I noticed a man a few hundred feet away. It was so strange; I thought I was seeing my nonno because he had the same exact walk as nonno! I knew this must be a relative coming to meet us. And it was! It was Zio Pietro, my grandfather's brother. He knew who we were immediately without an introduction. (That is the way it is in Italy. Relatives whom I have never met, or friends that I have not seen for years, all have this uncanny intuition, they know who you are immediately!)

Zio Pietro's son drove the car, and within five minutes, we arrived at my grandfather's vineyard. It was like something out of a dream for me! Here I was, finally meeting this cast of characters whom my grandparents had talked about so many times. My great aunts and uncles and some of their children and their children's children, they all stood before me!

The vineyard had three villas connected to each other. My grandfather's three remaining brothers Mario, Pietro, and Enrico lived there in separate houses with their wives. Some of the villas had separate apartment dwellings so their children and families could stay when they came for a visit. Zia Annina lived in another house on the other side of town with her husband Antonio. I had such an eerie feeling when I first met her. She was the youngest of the family, but she resembled, in such an uncanny way, the oldest sister, Zia Maria, who had immigrated to the United States and had passed on a few years before. She had the same walk as Zia Maria, the same mannerisms; it was as if Zia Maria had been reincarnated for me!

I stayed at Zio Mario's house, which was the villa in the center of the grounds. That first night Zia Anna, Mario's wife, made a wonderful dinner consisting of frittata with artichoke; zucchini imbotito; pasta with pecorino cheese produced there, at the vineyard, from the sheep's milk and, of course, wine produced at the vineyard. For dessert, we had a torta di mele, a type of apple pie that was, at the same time, sort of like a custard.

During my visit, I learned so many things about my family, interesting stories that I had never heard about life in Tagliacozza. There was so much family history that I never knew. My great-grandfather was killed by German soldiers when he refused to give the hungry occupying army his pigs. The Germans shot him dead at the end of the driveway, there, while my great-aunt, Ferdinanda, watched in horror.

My great-grandfather, or bis-nonno, had always had a keen sense of caring for his family. When the economic situation in Italy was horrible (many years before the war), my bis-nonno went to America looking to make his fortune. He had thirteen children to support, and there was no work in Italy. He found work building the Brooklyn Bridge in New York City. He stayed until he finished his work, all the while sending money back to his wife and children. Great-grandfather didn't like America, though, and he didn't want to bring his wife and kids there. So, when the work was done, he decided to return home.

When he arrived home, he recounted his adventures in America. His stories about how big America was and all the things going on there intrigued my grandfather and his oldest sister, Maria. They listened to their father's tales with fascination, more impressed than anybody else by these stories. Maria, the eldest sibling, eventually moved to America with her intended husband. Nonno followed her when he was only fourteen years old. Even at the age of fourteen, he dreamed of making money, which was in short supply in Italy. My great-grandfather had invested some of the money that he made purchasing land, but there was not always enough food and other necessities to go around. Also, there was no work in sight!

So my grandfather was determined to travel to America, to South Philadelphia, to live with his sister Maria, who was already settled there and had agreed to be his sponsor. Zio Mario still can hear my grandfather arguing with his father about how he wanted to go to America where he was sure he would become rich. My great-grandfather tried to discourage him. And my great grandmother, she was beside herself. She worried that she would never see her son again! But, stubbornness is a trait that is passed down from generation to generation in Tagliacozzo. Once the people there make their minds up to do something, they do it! And, so, off my grandfather went! Nonno had never told us what a heart-wrenching decision this was for his parents.

Nonno eventually found work in Michigan building tracks for the railroads. He worked hard, but knew Michigan was not for him. After earning a bit of money, he returned to South Philadelphia, settled into the close-knit Italian community there, and met my grandmother. They were from two different parts of Italy, he from the region of Abruzzi, she from Molise. At one time, Abruzzi and Molise were one and the same. Molise separated from Abruzzi and became an independent region in the 1960s. So, as far as my grandparents were concerned, they were really from the same region, although different ends of it. Because of this, they had in common the traditions and foods of their regions.

SUGO PER PASTA

1 pound fresh, ripe, plum tomatoes (or canned if fresh are not available)
2 tablespoons extra virgin, cold pressed olive oil or virgin olive oil
2 cloves garlic, peeled
1 slice of onion
3 basil leaves
Pinch of fine salt to taste

Filet the tomatoes cutting them into thin wedges and eliminating the seeds.
Place 2 tablespoons of olive oil in a large saucepan and add the garlic cloves and the slice of onion;
Lightly sauté, taking care not to burn the onion or garlic.
The garlic and onion should start to become a light, golden color in 1-2 minutes.

Then, add the tomato wedges.
Let the tomatoes boil down till almost no liquid remains.
Once they are cooked to a good consistency, add the basil.
Take the sauce off the burner.
The sauce is now ready to have pasta added to it.

CROSTINI PER ZUPPA (SOUP CROUTONS)

12 eggs
12 tablespoons flour
12 tablespoons Parmigiana cheese or grated cheese
¼ pound Italian ham (optional)
1 small ball mozzarella cheese (cut into chunks)
2 tablespoons parsley (dried or fresh)
2 tablespoons olive oil

Pour all the ingredients into a bowl.
Grease a cookie sheet with olive oil.
Pour the frittata mixture into the sheet and bake it in the oven at 350 degrees F for 15 minutes.
Then, remove it from the oven.
Let it cool and cut it into small squares, crouton size.

Use this to top stracciatella, Italian wedding soup, and many other soups as well.

CHAPTER 11
THE FORNO

The forno, or bakery, that I go to has been around for years. Everyone in town knows where this bakery is, even though there are no signs on it and it is not brightly decorated with neon. You walk through a doorway hung with strings of beads to enter this unassuming store. The forno lets its wares speak for it.

The forno's specialty is scrumptious potato bread, which is crusty on the outside and dense on the inside. Potatoes are produced in this region, and there is a type of potato that is especially suited for flour for bread. The forno also makes red pizza, white pizza (my favorite pizza with potatoes), as well as some sweets such as taralli and plain biscotti. Forno means oven, and it really refers to an oven used for dough. The bakers are connoisseurs of dough making, whether it is for pizza or bread. If you time your visit just right, when the bread or pizza comes out of the oven, you'll want to stay for a few minutes and just dine on the aroma!

One day we were heading home late and did not have any ideas for dinner. Since we were both tired, we decided to prepare a simple panino or sandwich. We stopped at the forno around the corner and bought some fresh bread. The forno bakes bread and pizza all day long, and if you time your arrival right, you can purchase bread hot and fresh from the oven. (Usually, the forno is so busy that even if the bread is not fresh out of the oven, chances are it was not baked longer than an hour ago.) So the bread just happened to be coming out of the oven when we arrived.

In Italy, you usually buy bread and pizza by weight and the standard measure that you are given is one kilogram, or about two pounds. Instead, I asked the baker's wife for the specific quantity of bread that I wanted, that is, just enough for four small slices. The bread was hot, and its perfume was tantalizing. Also, the bakery was about to close for the day, and, so, I knew the shopkeeper wanted to sell me a whole loaf instead of just a small piece. As she sliced the bread, she told me that I would want to eat more of it once I tasted it. Was I sure that I didn't want the whole thing? She was right when I tasted the bread, later at home, I wished we had bought more!

When we got home, we assembled the panini combining the fresh, hot bread with sliced fresh mozzarella, sliced tomatoes, and fresh basil with a dash of extra virgin olive oil. That had to be the most delicious sandwich I have ever eaten. I can still taste that panino.

Italians love their food, but I think that they take it for granted. When I eat a freshly baked piece of bread, or pizza, or cornetto–the Italian version of a croissant–I am in heaven! Sometimes, I have to shut my eyes for a few moments and savor the taste, because, when baked fresh, the taste of bread is such a real, and pure, taste. It is a flavor that, in the U.S., is considered gourmet or out of the ordinary.

But such aromas and tastes are commonplace for Italians. They have grown up with this quality of food all around them. The only way I can get food that is this delicious and fresh is if I, my mom, or one of my aunts, cook the meal with ingredients from the Italian market in Philadelphia or Brooklyn. So, it is difficult to explain to Italians why we Americans go crazy when we taste a morsel of their wonderful food.

And, I must admit that, when I cook in Italy, the food tastes much better than when I cook the same dish in the United States. Is it something in the air? No, actually I think it is just that the quality of the ingredients is so much higher in Italy than what is imported into the States.

Even for a simple panino the quality and freshness of the ingredients matter. Here's the way to make a wonderful panino.

THE BASIC, WONDERFUL PANINO (SANDWICH ON ITALIAN BUNS)

2 ripe tomatoes-preferably ripened on the vine-cut into thin slices
1 pound fresh mozzarella cheese*
Extra virgin, cold pressed olive oil**
Small handful of fresh basil leaves, washed and patted dry with a paper towel***
Dash of salt

* You must get fresh mozzarella. If it is fresh, it is kept in water.
You should also find out how long ago it was produced. Always remember, the fresher the better.

** Olive oil should be in a dark glass bottle.
If it is sold in a clear glass bottle, it may not be fresh because light makes olive oil oxidize.

*** If you cannot get fresh basil, please do not use dried.
Try fresh arugula or baby spinach leaves instead, but for the best taste, try your hardest to find that fresh basil.

Place the olive oil in an olive oil can with a long, thin spout.
Put a fine line of olive oil on each of the bread slices.

Cut the mozzarella into slices about ¼-inch thick-not too thin, or the mozzarella will crumble.
Place these cheese slices on top of the bread.
Then, put the tomato slices on top of mozzarella cheese.
Tear up the basil leaves and put them on top of the tomatoes.
Add a pinch of salt, to your liking, and then dribble that wonderful olive oil on top-not too much, about 2 teaspoons or so.

Top with the other slice of bread and cut the sandwich in half.

This panino is best when served with a glass of red wine such as Montepulciano D'Abruzzo, a good Chianti, or a red Lacrima di Christi.

This is an excellent sandwich to take with you if you are going on a hike or walk, or spending the day at the beach. We take this sandwich and a big bottle of mineral water when we spend the day hiking in the mountains. But it is best eaten as soon as possible and definitely on the same day as it is made.

OUR MEMORIES IN ITALY

XII GIORNATA DEL FRANCOBOLLO

CHAPTER 12
MEMORIES OF AVEZZANO

It was a meal prepared by one of my cousins in Avezzano that inspired me to learn more about cooking. Of course, I had learned to cook some basic dishes from my mom and my grandmother, and I had always enjoyed eating Italian foods. But, I had never taken notice of the art of cooking Italian foods before that evening. I felt almost ashamed that my cousin, who was almost the same age as I was, could cook such a wonderful meal and that I had never really taken the time to learn how to make so much as a béchamel sauce.

Avezzano is about twenty minutes away from Tagliacozzo, where the family vineyards are. My cousin lives in Avezzano with her husband, an attorney. It was their daughter, a college student, who prepared the dinner on our first night at their home. It was a dinner that a professional chef would be proud of and I came to see that, in Italy, cooking happened at a more sophisticated level whether it was in a restaurant or a private home.

Most Italians do not learn to cook at a professional cooking school. They learn from the family and friends they grow up around, people who consider cooking an art and the act of cooking as creating and not just throwing ingredients together. Italians' lives revolve around good foods. My grandmothers, aunts, and mother all cook well, but our lifestyles do not hold food in such an important light as it enjoys in Italy.

As I spent more time in Italy, I had more and more dinners prepared by unbelievable chefs, housewives, students, even my uncles turned out to be experts in the kitchen!

Gnocchi in béchamel sauce was the dinner my cousin prepared for us that evening, and here it is for you to prepare as I learned to prepare it. I had always thought that gnocchi were cooked with a tomato sauce, or sugo, but my cousin taught me that this did not necessarily have to be the case.

By the way, this recipe is served well with a good dry and light white wine such as Trebbiano d'Abruzzi.

GNOCCHI DI PATATE CON SUGO DI POMODORO
(POTATO DUMPLINGS WITH TOMATO SAUCE)

Gnocchi
2 pounds potatoes
2 cups flour
1 egg
Salt to taste

Fill a large pot with water and put in a pinch of gross salt.
When the water is boiling rapidly, put in the potatoes.
When the potatoes are cooked-test for doneness by seeing if a fork will easily go through a potato
Drain them in a colander and peel them while still hot.

Put the boiled and peeled potatoes through a potato ricer or masher.
Quickly add in the flour, egg, and a pinch of salt.
Mix all the ingredients well, by hand, until they are blended together thoroughly.

Make the dough into one log that is the thickness of about two fingers held together.
Sprinkle flour on a wooden board and place the dough on it.
Work the dough with your hands and, then, divide it into two "logs"–each the thickness of one finger.
Cut off small "pea size" gnocchi.
To give them a gnocchi form, place 2 fingertips on a piece of dough and roll it gently.
When all the gnocchi are prepared, sprinkle them with flour. (If possible, use semolina flour.)
Let the gnocchi stand while you prepare the sugo, or sauce.

BÉCHAMEL SAUCE

This sauce is used more in the north of Italy than the tomato sauce from the south.

2 cups milk
2 tablespoons flour
Salt to taste
Dash of nutmeg

Place the ingredients in a saucepan over low heat and let them thicken, stirring constantly.

Do not allow the sauce to burn.

SUGO DI POMODORO

1 pound fresh plum tomatoes
or 1 16-ounce can plum tomatoes
3 tablespoons olive oil
1 tablespoon onion, chopped finely
2 cloves garlic
Fresh basil leaves
Salt to taste
Freshly grated Parmigiana-reggiano cheese

Place oil in a frying pan and add in onions that have been chopped finely and 2 cloves garlic.
Sauté the onions and garlic until they begin to turn a golden color.
Then add the tomatoes.
Let the sugo cook over low heat, stirring regularly with a wooden spoon.
Add a pinch of salt.
After 20 minutes, most of the liquid should be absorbed and the tomatoes should be concentrated.
Tear, or chop into pieces, two fresh, washed, basil leaves and add them to the tomato sauce.
Stir gently.
Cover the sauce and remove it from the heat.

Place the gnocchi gently into a large pot of rapidly boiling water.
The gnocchi will first fall to the bottom—after a short time, they will begin to slowly rise to the surface of the water.
When they have all risen to the top, quickly, and gently, place them in a colander to drain the water off of them.
Run some cold water over them while they are still in the colander.
Place the gnocchi in the pan with the sauce and gently toss them.

Place servings of gnocchi on individual plates and freshly grate the Parmigiana cheese on to each plate.

PART V
Seconds

Italian

FRESH

71

Now comes the part of the meal that everyone has been waiting for! This is where the guests really dig into their cena, and the chef has a chance to shine! Any of these dishes can be served with any of the contorni listed in Part III.

And don't forget to include your choice of a fine wine. In Italy, almost any wine is a good wine, but the best is the wine that people make from the grapes right in their own homes.

As you savor the succulent flavors of an Italian main course, you will, without a doubt, also have the benefit of exciting conversations all around you. Let me share some over-dinner stories with you for you to enjoy with your choice of secondi.

CHAPTER 13
ALLA SPIAGGIA

In the hot, desert-like months of August, we usually spend at least a week on the beaches of Pescara. Pescara is an inviting part of Abruzzo, the region that produces the wonderful wines of Abruzzo, Montepulciano, and Trebbiano. In the summertime, fruit vendors sell the white grapes, which are grown here, by the crate for eating and/or winemaking. If the summer weather is good and hot, without too much rain, the stores will just be overflowing with these grapes.

The beaches are in the newer section of Pescara, but tourists also find their way to the old part of the city where one of Pescara's most well-known residents once lived. Gabriello D'Annunzio was a famous poet and writer of the early 1900s and quite the ladies man. The house where he was born as well as a small museum dedicated to D'Annunzio remain.

Italy is fully of interesting characters. In fact, some could even be your neighbors. When we are in Pescara, we stay at our condo on the beach. However, we often visit some of the agriturismi in the hills of Pescara to eat dinner. One summer evening, when we were returning to our condo after dining out, we became trapped in a broken elevator. Normally, the claustrophobic person that I am avoids the elevator, after all the building is only three stories high. But that evening, Alfonso talked me into using the elevator, and, sure enough, there we were, stuck inside an elevator that was going nowhere.

That is when we met Antonio Del Poeta, a charming old man who served as the superintendent of the building. His name as poetic as he was. Antonio was a slight man, frail, but ever spirited, and so proud to have rescued us. When he saw that I was quite shaken by the incident, he invited us to his condo in the building and showed us around. The decor was something out of 1960 Italy, and immediately, I was enchanted with Antonio's home and Antonio himself. He proudly showed us a declaration on the wall, which stated that he was a cavaliere. A cavaliere is the Italian version of a knight, and this honor is presented to one who has done something honorable or has had a special achievement of some kind. The friendly and gracious Antonio invited us to stop by one day for dinner and assured us that his wife always prepared something special to eat.

The time sped by, and we never got to have dinner with the Del Poetas. Oh, how I wish we had! The next year, when we arrived in Pescara, there was a sign in front of the building announcing the death of Antonio Del Poeta. It was strange. I hadn't really known this man, yet I was filled with sadness at his passing. In our brief experience with Antonio, he had shown again that he was indeed a cavaliere; he had shown compassion and offered friendship to strangers in an elevator. I wished we had taken him up on his dinner invitation.

Pescara has a wonderful fresh fish market, and you will hear people on the beach all day discussing their recipe for a type of paella with an Italian flair. So, if you have spent the day on the beach listening to people planning their paella dinners with passion, I might add that your mouth will be watering for that dish of fresh seafood and risotto. Our favorite thing to do after a day at the beach is to make a delicious paella for dinner. Of course, you have to make sure you get to the fish market early so that you get your pick of fresh fish for this dish. Put your fresh fish in salted water and refrigerate it, and then you're off to the beach.

BRODO DI PESCARA (ITALIAN PAELLA FROM PESCARA)

You will need fresh fish, bought and cleaned at the marketplace. Leave these to soak in salted water for a few hours before cooking them up in this Italian form of paella.

Fresh mussels
Fresh clams (the really small ones are the best)
Extra Virgin olive oil
Onion
Dried peppers

In heated olive oil, sauté thinly sliced onion and dried hot peppers.
Allow the onions to turn golden then remove them from the heat and cool them.
Put the onion mixture in a food processor and chop it up finely.

In a large pan, heat enough olive oil to coat the bottom of the pan and put in the onion mixture.
Add steamed mussels and clams, stir, and let them cook to absorb the flavor of the onion mixture for about 5 minutes. (A mixture that is lightly sautéed like this is called a soffritto.)

Serve this dish as a second course.

CHAPTER 14

NERONE

It was a perfect day for a stroll up the Via Veneto in Rome. The clear skies and summer sun caressed the Via Veneto with its outdoor cafés and people simply enjoying life. There is a plaque dedicating this street to director Federico Fellini, who so skillfully captured its spirit in his famous La Dolce Vita. If you close your eyes for a minute, you can just imagine everything in black and white, as the film was, and the paparazzi racing up and down the street at night. At one time, the Via Veneto was the hot spot for the "glitterati."

On this day the excitement was happening at a gallery displaying work from the Studio Nerone in Reggio–Emilia, and I had an invitation to the exposition. Studio Nerone houses the famous Italian artist, Sergio Terzi, whose nickname and professional name is Nerone. He took this as his moniker because of the similarities between himself and Emperor Nerone of ancient Rome who is known for, among other things, having burned buildings in his trail. While Emperor Nerone gave up after his palace burned down, the artist Nerone rebuilt his studio more than once after fires, and then resumed his work.

Nerone paints in primitive style and is well known for having studied under the tutelage of another of Italy's famous painters who is simply known as Ligabue. Ligabue's personality was compared to Vincent Van Gogh's; the word "mad" was likely to be mentioned when talking about Ligabue.

As we entered the gallery where the exposition was being held, the first thing that caught my eye was the striking color of a set of sunflower paintings. These were Nerone's work. They captured the vibrant blues and yellows that I always think of when I think of the Italian landscape in the summertime. However, Nerone does not only paint landscapes. He also is famous for his paintings of the famous, from opera singer Luciano Pavarotti to Zucchero, one of Italy's best known modern recording artists.

I had just come from doing a fashion show in the center of Rome earlier that day and the designer had allowed me to borrow one of the outfits from the show to wear to the art exposition. My blouse was a vibrant orange color, and I almost felt as if I had stepped out of a Nerone painting. When I was introduced to Nerone, I learned that he already knew who I was (at that time, I was modeling frequently in Italy). In fact, I had been invited to the exposition so that Nerone could ask me to be his next subject. He wanted to paint my portrait for his next exhibit. Of course, I was flattered. Nerone said that the people whose portraits he paints are all acquaintances of his and that he would love to give me my painting as a gift once he was finished exhibiting it.

Later that day, we discussed how he would do the painting. I had a busy schedule, and his studio was in the middle of the fields of Reggio-Emilia, a province in the north of Italy. That region is famous for many things including the Parmigiano-Reggiano cheese and Prosciutto di Parma, a delicious Italian cured ham. Since it was not likely that my schedule would include Reggio-Emilia in the near future, Nerone decided that it would be best to paint my portrait using photos of me. So, the photographer at the gallery that day took some pictures of me at Nerone's request.

Surely he would forget about this, I thought, as we left the gallery that day.

Four months later, however, a large envelope arrived at my office in the United States. In it were the pictures the photographer had taken that day and a large photo of the painting that Nerone had done of me! In his letter, he noted that he would be exhibiting my painting at Spazio Italia, a gallery in Soho in New York City that promoted Italian artists. Even more exciting was the news that the painting also would be exhibited in the Metropolitan Museum of Art in Manhattan! Nerone had been selected to receive an award honoring artistic people who have promoted Italian arts and culture. This award is presented every year in honor of Columbus Day. Nerone was going to be a recipient of the award along with director Franco Zeffirelli, actor Robert De Niro, and some other artists local to Manhattan.

I quickly got in touch with Nerone and synchronized our schedules so that I could be there for these important events. I also assumed that he would give me my painting after these exhibits, as he had promised.

Communicating with Nerone is always a little difficult as he speaks with an accent from his region. Even though Italian is one language, it has many regional differences just as the foods and aspects of culture. Since some of my family is from an area that is not far from Naples, and I am a fan of the old traditional Italian songs and operas which were written in Neapolitan dialect, I understand very well when someone speaks with a Neapolitan accent or even uses the Neapolitan dialect. I also understand the dialect of Abruzzo since that is where I live. Naples is in the south of Italy, and Abruzzo is considered part of the south as well.

Nerone comes from the north of Italy where the people enjoy an almost completely different culture from the south. They speak with a different dialect and eat many different foods. One important difference between the south and the north is that, in northern Italian cuisine, most dishes are made with butter instead of olive oil.

Nerone's region also is known for the Po River. If you are American and see the Po River, you will think of it as a large creek, and not a river at all. But for the people who live near it, the Po is an important river. Many poems and songs have been written about the power of the mighty Po River. Many of Nerone's paintings also reflect the Po River. The Po's power lies in the fact that it has a strong influence on the weather conditions of the area and frequently causes fog. It is dangerous to drive a car in the area at night because of the fog, and there are rarely any lights on the streets. So, the Po River, it is said, actually has its own personality. If it is angry, it can produce fog or overflow. If it is happy, it can remain calm and pristine.

The cuisine around the Po River is also distinct and well known.

In his late teens, Nerone took up carpentry. By the time he was in his early twenties, he had gathered enough money to start a furniture studio. He and his co-workers expanded into a large empty church where they created many handcrafted pieces. One day the church burned down to the ground taking everything, including all the furniture. After this catastrophe, some in the town began to call Sergio Terzi "Nerone." The nickname stuck and became his professional name.

Nerone not only had to support his younger siblings, but also a wife and small son. He worked at making furniture feverishly during the weeks and on the weekends as well! Soon he found a partner and they opened a commercial furniture studio. The business thrived and the partners branched out, opening a nightclub in the center of a nearby town called Villarota. Unfortunately, Nerone's new success was short-lived. His partner began making investments that went bad, and soon the businesses floundered. With this turn of events, an angry Nerone sunk into despair. He turned to drinking alcohol as a solace and started spending more and more time in the local bars in the company of his drinking buddies. Soon, he found himself spending entire days drinking in a bar, and he teetered on the brink of suicide.

It was at this period in his life that he met the well-known painter, Ligabue. Ligabue was a "tortured soul" himself, as well as an alcoholic. But Nerone noticed that Ligabue transformed into a different person when he was in front of a palette. Painting was a sort of therapy for Ligabue, a way to release all of his torment and pain through the brilliant colors on the canvas. Soon, Ligabue convinced Nerone to do the same.

After a few months of study under Ligabue, Nerone won a prestigious award in Milan for one of his paintings. More and more, Nerone turned to his art as a way to work out his problems. He was becoming widely known and praised for his artistic abilities, and his paintings began to sell faster than he could create them! He won prize after prize for his paintings, and he established a studio and a workshop where he could work and where other artists could come and study with him just as he had studied with Ligabue. Nerone's work is now included in Italy's most important art catalogues, and he is recognized by many art critics throughout the world.

The one thing that always impressed me about Nerone is that he is a simple man. He likes living near nature surrounded, as he says, "with the beautiful colors of nature." He finds the flowers, the trees, the fields, the Po River, and the birds all so scenic. He told me that he could not become accustomed to having a concrete sidewalk under his feet and that he longed for green fields. He told me that even though New York is a wondrous city, it is not a place that he would find himself for any reason other than business. He needs the peace and tranquility of nature to live and for inspiration. He credits the beauty of nature for inspiring some of his works of art and also for the vivid colors that he uses to paint. The sun, he says, paints nature with its light. It makes colors more vivid and he tries to capture that vibrancy in his paintings.

Needless to say, Nerone's exhibits were a success in New York. I, too, received a certificate of recognition from the Metropolitan Museum of Art for promoting Italian culture. Even though I enjoyed spending time with Nerone and his assistants, I couldn't help but feel happy for him when it was time for him to leave New York and return home. Although I knew that he enjoyed exhibiting his paintings, I could not help but notice that he seemed somewhat uncomfortable in city surroundings. He felt "out of his element," he said. Nerone thrives on nature; it gives him his life force, and this was never more evident than during his time in New York. But when he left, he promised me, again, that when he was finished exhibiting my painting throughout Europe, he would give it to me as a gift.

I find it paradoxical that Italians who have given the world so many artistic masterpieces, often are most impressed by simple things. They find so much beauty in nature. They are an earthy people. Most Italians can speak for hours about the beauty of the sun, the clearness of the sky, the majesty of a mountain, or the personality of a body of water.

In America, we need many things to make a beautiful ambiance. But, in Italy, surround yourself with the sun at the top of a mountain and you have beauty, no furniture or ostentatious objects are necessary. It is so refreshing to see, when one is in Italy, the way that the beauty of nature is appreciated.

There are so many days that I find myself sitting on our terrace in Abruzzo, just staring out at the mountains and listening to the birds and the quiet around me, feeling the warmth of the sun, and also noticing how the sun does make the colors of nature so vivid. On these days, I think about what Nerone taught me about appreciating the beauty of nature. Sitting there, I can also imagine myself to be in a type of live painting.

Even though I was excited to know that my portrait was part of the exhibit he was showing throughout Europe, I was anxious to get my painting. So, I was ecstatic when Nerone called to let me know that he was finished exhibiting my painting and that I could finally have it! I was surprised to learn, however, that he wanted me to pick up the painting personally at his studio in the north of Italy. I was so excited that I immediately agreed, never considering once during our phone conversation, how I would handle the logistics of getting the painting home.

It would require driving the huge painting in my fiancé's itty-bitty Fiat from the Parma region where Nerone's studio was to my fiance's studio, in the center of Rome, and then flying it home to Philadelphia. I called my fiancé, Alfonso. He was excited about the painting and at the news of my impending visit; we immediately began planning our itinerary.

Nerone invited us to stay overnight at his friend's villa, which was around the corner from his house. There wasn't room at Nerone's home. He lives in a big complex with his entire family including his brothers and their wives and kids. (This is customary with some families, in Italy, that have large villas or complexes.)

Alfonso and I decided to turn the trip to pick up my painting into a chance to explore the towns and sights along the famous Po River. Alfonso was particularly excited about visiting the town of Marinella, which we had to pass through to get to our final destination of Gualtieri. Marinella was the home of the Ferrari plant and museum, which Alfonso was dying to see. We also stopped in Modena, the birthplace of Luciano Pavarotti and the place where balsamic vinegar is a regional specialty. We enjoyed the Lago del Gardo, which is not far from Lake Como. It is not as "touristy" or well known as Lake Como, but just as beautiful.

We had a wonderful journey into the north of Italy, and our stay with Nerone and his friends was unforgettable. Although bringing the painting back to Rome proved to be a bit of a challenge, it did make the journey back safely!

I will never forget Nerone or the experience of having a painting of myself in an art gallery for all to see. Even the journey to go and get the painting when the dream was all over, was a dream in itself.

TORTA DI RISO (PIE WITH RICE)

7 whole eggs
2 cups rice
¾ cup grated pecorino or grana padana cheese
½ cup butter
2 cups milk
Dash of pepper and salt
Flour

Cook the rice until it is al dente, about 15 minutes. Do not use instant rice.

In a casserole dish, beat the whole eggs and place melted butter and grated pecorino or grana padana cheese in with the eggs.
Then, add the rice and salt and pepper to taste. Add the milk to the rice mixture.

In another small bowl, prepare a dough from flour and water and let it stand.

Oil the bottom of a pan and cover it with dough. Place the rice mixture on the dough and then cover it with more dough.
Drizzle the top of the torta with olive oil.

Bake at 475 degrees F for 15 minutes, then lower the temperature to 400 degrees F for another 45 minutes.
Be sure not to let the pie become too dry and brown.
The crust on top should be golden.

While still warm, cut the torta into slices and serve.

POLPETTE (MEATBALLS)

1 pound ground meat made up the following way:
1/3 beef, 1/3 pork, 1/3 veal
¼ cup breadcrumbs (you can add more to make meatballs firm)
2 tablespoons locatelli or parmagiano cheese
2 eggs
Herbs and 1 teaspoon of fresh or dried parsley
Salt to taste (optional)

Mix all the above ingredients.
When they have been mixed well, form the ground meat into meatballs.

Coat a frying pan with about 3-4 teaspoons of olive oil.
You may dip the meatballs into breadcrumbs before frying.
You may also bake the meatballs.

Fry the meatballs, or bake them, until they are brown on the outside.

PEPPERONI IMBOTTITI (STUFFED PEPPERS)

1½ cups cannelloni beans
½ cup white onion, minced
2 teaspoons fresh garlic, minced finely
½ cup extra virgin cold pressed olive oil
1 can (6 ounces) tuna packed in olive oil
juice from 1 fresh lemon squeezed
1/3 cup freshly chopped parsley
8 fresh peppers
(to make this dish colorful, you can choose an assortment of colors for the peppers, if they are in season)

If you are using dried beans you must first soak them overnight-or for at least 12 hours-covered with water.
Then, drain them and place them in a pot.
Cover them with cold water and cook them for approximately 30 minutes or until they are tender.

Once the beans are cooked, drain them.
Place, in a large bowl, the beans, olive oil, garlic, onions, lemon juice, and salt to taste.

Take the whole peppers; cut off their tops and put them aside.
Scoop out the inside of the peppers and take out the seeds and pulp.
To get the peppers to stand, you can cut off a little piece from the bottom so they sit on a flat surface and can remain upright.

Stuff the peppers with the bean mixture you made.

You can serve these peppers raw as an antipasto or a light meal.
Serve them at home or take them to the beach, in the summertime, as a light lunch.

TORTA SALATA (SALTED CAKE)

1 pound small zucchini
3 fresh small onions cut into very thin slices
½ clove garlic crushed
½ cup of water and ½ cup milk, mixed together
4 tablespoons flour
2 eggs
4 tablespoons grated parmigiano cheese
Extra virgin oil
Salt and pepper to taste

Cut the zucchini into thin slices, sprinkle it lightly with salt, and let it stand for 20 minutes.

Then beat the eggs with the flour. Add in the water and milk mixture. Until a smooth dough is formed.

Rinse the zucchini to take out the salt and dry it with a paper towel.
Add the zucchini, onions, grated cheese, and garlic to the dough.

Butter a pie pan and place the zucchini dough mixture in it.
Drizzle it with some olive oil and bake it at 400 degrees F until golden.
Serve warm covered with grated cheese.

BRACIOLE TOSCANA (TUSCAN PORK STEAKS)

4 thin slices of pork used for braciole, or fast fry steaks.
(These should be 1/3 pound each, no bones and thinly cut slices.)
1 clove garlic
a dash of anise seeds, crushed
1 glass of Chianti red wine
Salt and pepper to taste

Salt and pepper the 4 slices of pork.
Place them in a non-stick frying pan with a clove of crushed garlic and anise seeds, crushed as well.
Let the meat become golden; then add the wine.
Cover the pan and continue cooking the meat on low heat until the wine is almost totally burned off and meat is well done. Remove from heat and serve.
Serve hot.

Italian

ROMANCE

When partaking of an Italian meal, everything becomes more lighthearted at dessert time. Whether it's because everyone around the table is almost sated and becoming somewhat more relaxed or whether it is because it's almost a form of disrespect to not enjoy the light, refreshing tastes of the dolci (or sweets) that everyone becomes less serious and conversation turns to happy and funny stories about friends, family, and any strangers who happen to pop to mind!

Let me join in the chit-chat while you enjoy one of these wonderful dolci!

CHAPTER 15
CIAO, MIO AMORE

How did I meet Alfonso?

It was a Saturday night, and I was visiting a quaint little town in the mountains of Abruzzo. I had heard of this town since I was a little girl. It often was the topic of conversation during Sunday dinners at my grandparents' house in South Philadelphia and during visits to the Italian market on Saturday mornings when I would accompany nonno to choose the grapes for his wine and the tomatoes for nonna's sugo.

That night it seemed as if everyone in the town had turned out for one big party in the piazza. Piazza means square in Italian, and every town, no matter how small it is, has one. It is usually in a central point in town, and most of the time the town church is in the center of the piazza or nearby.

On this night, the piazza was a romantic setting with the church steeple so proud and the mountains all around us. Everyone was happy and laughing and asking me questions about America. They were fascinated with all things American. Several people even tried a few English words.

Alfonso simply walked up to me and began to talk. Apparently, his parents knew my cousin, so mostly we talked about my family in Italy. I had come to the piazza with my cousin and brother. That small connection made me feel comfortable when talking with him.

Small town living in Italy is just that way. If you grow up in a small town, you can be sure that everyone knows almost everything about you and your family.

As the festivities in the piazza wound down, we all agreed to meet at the pizza restaurant at 9 p.m. for dinner. (This late hour is actually a typical time for eating dinner on a Saturday night in Italy. Everyone usually leaves the piazza by 7:45 to eat dinner or to get ready to go out for dinner.) Since my cousin and brother were walking home with other friends, Alfonso asked if he could escort me back to my cousin's house. It was quite old-fashioned and charming.

My cousin's house was only five minutes from the piazza so it was a quick walk. On the way, Alfonso and I talked, partly in English and partly in Italian, about many things. (Our conversations today take the same form; he likes to practice his English and I like to practice my Italian. So, we have invented our own type of language wherein we speak half English, half Italian.) He walked me to the door, greeted my cousins, and confirmed the time we would all be meeting at the restaurant.

When my cousins and I arrived at the restaurant, I was surprised at how many people were there. It seemed like the whole piazza had decided to join us. We all sat at a big, long table. Alfonso had reserved a place for me next to him. The restaurant was famous for pizza made in big squares and that had many different toppings. We decided to order five different toppings, and everyone tasted each of them.

Conversation was quite loud at our table of twenty-five people, but it was a Saturday night in the summer and everyone was in high spirits. Afterwards, a group of us decided to move on to a coffee bar for coffee and aperitifs. The group included my cousin and her boyfriend, two of their friends, my brother, Alfonso, and me.

Amid the beautiful music and the fast-paced conversation at the coffee bar, Alfonso asked me out on a date. He invited me to go sightseeing with him the next morning. I eagerly said yes. We agreed to meet at the piazza, near the main coffee bar in town, at 10 a.m.

I was at the coffee bar at 10 a.m., but there was no Alfonso. I waited for an hour, and still he did not show. My heart dropped, Alfonso had seemed so sincere when I talked to him and I could not believe he would stand me up! I decided to do my own sightseeing in town. At noon, I went to the piazza, and there he was! He ran up to me and apologized, explaining that he had overslept. (He could not call me. This was in the days before cell phones became popular so neither of us had one.) He apologized many times over and promised to take me to a wonderful restaurant that night to make up for his tardiness.

The restaurant Alfonso took me to was well known in Abruzzo. It was popular for its special pasta made with tartufi, or truffles. (Truffles are found in that region, and many specialty dishes are made with them.) We had a wonderfully romantic dinner. The food, the music, the wine, and the mountains in the background all came together with the cool crisp night air to create a setting so lovely that it could have been a scene in a movie. And, there I was, the love interest of that beautiful scene!

We talked about seeing each other again. Alfonso promised to visit me in America, and we exchanged phone numbers and addresses. When we arrived at my cousin's door, I didn't want to go inside. We had had so much fun discussing our families' histories; both of our great-grandfathers had briefly gone to the United States in the late 1800's to earn a living before returning home to Italy. (My great-grandfather worked on the construction of the Brooklyn Bridge, and his great-grandfather opened a bar in San Francisco during the California Gold Rush).

The next day, my brother and I boarded a train headed for Rome. When we arrived in Rome, we were supposed to change trains and continue to another cousin's home south of there. But, I could not go on! Something just came over me, and I told my brother that I couldn't leave. I needed to go back to Abruzzo! When we got off the train, I telephoned my cousin and asked if we could come back and stay for a few more days.

She immediately said, "It's for love, but, of course, you can come back." She agreed to meet us at the train station.

When we arrived, my cousin and her family were so happy to see us. You see, Italians thrive on romance and love. They were so happy to be a part of this, a romance, and that it was love that drew me back to their town.

They encouraged me to call Alfonso immediately and let him know I had come back. Needless to say, Alfonso and I spent the next few days on a whirlwind together. I visited his office in town. We took long hikes in the mountains in the afternoons, and we went out to dinner every night. After dinner, we would make a trip to the local gelato, or ice cream, parlor and then walk around the piazza with our treats!

When the demands of my schedule called and it came time for me to return to the States, I was sad. Again, Alfonso promised to come to the U.S. to see me and meet my family. He did just that the next month. And, as they say, "the rest is history."

FRAGOLE CON LIMONE (STRAWBERRIES WITH LEMON)

1 pound fresh strawberries
1 lemon (grown organically)
3 tablespoons sugar (to your taste)
A handful of fresh mint leaves

Wash the strawberries and hull them with a small knife.

If you are using the baby strawberries, or fragolini, you do not have to cut them.

If you are using the normal-sized strawberries, cut each strawberry in half. Squeeze your lemon over the halved strawberries and sprinkle on the sugar.

Refrigerate for one hour and then taste the strawberries after all the flavors have had a chance to marinade.

Divide the strawberries into 4-5 dessert cups, garnish them with mint leaves, and serve them cold, right from the refrigerator.

MINTED PEARS WITH PARMIGIANO-REGGIANO CHEESE

2 large Bartlett or bosc pears; these should be ripe but firm
1 slice parmigiano-reggiano cheese
8 slices fresh mint
Balsamic vinegar

Wash and peel the pears.
Slice each pear into 6 slices, eliminating the seeds and core near the seeds.
Crumble the parmigiano reggiano cheese into small chunks.

Take 4 small serving dishes.
On one side of each dish, layer 3 slices of pear with a slice of mint in between each slice.
On the other side of the dish, arrange 3 or 4 small chunks of parmigiano reggiano cheese and sprinkle a small drop of balsamic vinegar on top of the cheese.
Do not saturate the cheese with the vinegar, but just slightly wet it to give the cheese a hint of flavor of the balsamic.

CARAMELE DI NOCE

¼ cup flour
2 tablespoons cold water
3 tablespoons margarine or butter
For frying safflower, corn, canola, peanut or sunflower oil (approx. 1 cup)

Filling:
½ cup finely ground nuts (almonds, pecans, walnuts, or hazelnuts–use a mixture of one or more of these nuts)
½ cup + 3 tablespoons sugar
1 teaspoon ground cinnamon

In a bowl, mix the flour and butter together with your hands until it resembles coarse crumbs.
Slowly add water and mix until a ball is formed. (Don't overmix.)
Refrigerate this dough for 2 hours.

In another small bowl, mix together the walnuts and 3 tablespoons of sugar.
In another small bowl, mix together the ½ cup sugar and cinnamon.

On a lightly floured surface, roll the dough into a 10-inch square.
Cut the dough lengthwise into 5-inch strips and cut each strip into 5 squares.
Lightly brush each square with melted butter and place 1 teaspoon of walnut mixture in its center.
Then, roll each one "jelly roll" style. Pinch the ends closed and twist each end.
Gather any leftover dough and roll into other caramelle.

In a deep, heavy frying pan, heat the oil.
Fry the caramelle one at a time until they are golden brown.
They can also be baked at 375 degrees °F in the oven for 10 minutes.
Remove them from the oven, or frying pan, and drain them.
While they are still hot, roll the caramelle in the cinnamon-sugar mixture.

PANETTONE BREAD PUDDING

2 cups milk
2 eggs
½ teaspoon vanilla
½ cup sugar
Dried panettone cubes (if the panettone is not dried, place it in an oven or toaster for a few minutes)

Blend all liquid ingredients together with sugar.
Arrange panettone cubes in the bottom of a glass pan.
Pour the liquid mixture over the panettone and bake at 350 degrees F for 30 minutes.

Sprinkle baked bread pudding with powdered sugar, or brown sugar, on top.

This can also be served with vanilla ice cream, whip cream, et cetera

CHAPTER 16
FRESH FRUIT AND FAMILY FAVORITES

Nonna loved Christmas, Easter, and Thanksgiving, because on those special days, our large family could be counted on to gather in celebration. She and Nonno missed being surrounded by family daily, as they had been back in Italy. They loved sharing a grand holiday dinner with all the aunts, uncles, cousins, great-aunts, great-uncles, children, and grandchildren in the States.

No Italian holiday dinner would be complete without the Macedonia, or fruit salad. In Italy, it is customary to end almost any meal with fresh fruit or Macedonia. It is a healthy custom.

When I am in Italy, I delight in making my Macedonia because it brings back memories of family dinners at Nonna's house in Philadelphia or gatherings at Nonno's vineyard with my great-aunts, uncles, and cousins. That is the way it is with Italian food. It nourishes us in both body and spirit. It is why we Italians enjoy cooking. We serve up not only delicious food, but sweet memories.

For me, the making of Macedonia is a delightful experience because it is created from the fresh fruits of Italy (except in winter, when I must use some of the fruits I conserved in summer). The best Macedonia is made by following the rule that all great Italian cooks know, use only fruits that are "in season." In the summer in Italy, there are so many fruits from which to choose! Each month I try to emphasize the fresh fruits that are in season. This will give my Macedonia the purest taste. If you cannot find fresh fruit, and really want the next best thing, use freshly conserved or frozen fruit.

If you really want to make an authentic Macedonia, you must use a fresh lemon from Sorrento. The lemons of Sorrento are produced in the summer and are so sweet you can slice them up and eat them like oranges. But I understand that we cannot all get our fruit from Sorrento. So for the Macedonia, any lemon will do. The important thing is that you use lemon, because it brings out the flavors of all the fruit.

MACEDONIA

(You can substitute fresh fruits that are in season for the fruits given here.)
1½ cups strawberries
2 large sweet oranges
2 large red or golden delicious apples (peeled, cored, and cut into thick slices, about ¼-inch thick)
2 pears (whatever variety is in season) (peeled, cored, and cut like the apples)
2 bananas peeled and sliced into ¼-inch round pieces
1 fresh cantaloupe, with skin and seeds removed and cut into ¼-inch cubes (you can substitute this with any melon that is in season)
Juice of one fresh lemon
¼ cup sugar
¼ cup maraschino liqueur or red wine
Fresh mint leaves for garnish

Combine all of the fruit in a decorative bowl.

Mix, in a small bowl, the juice of the lemon, the sugar, and the liqueur or red wine.
Pour the lemon mixture over the fruit and stir gently, taking care not to break the fruit pieces, until all the fruit is covered in the mixture.
Cover the Macedonia and refrigerate it for at least 2 hours before serving.
Taste the Macedonia, and, if you would like to add a touch more sugar, do so now. (If you do not want to add more sugar, go ahead and garnish the Macedonia with some gelato to make the fruit taste sweeter.)
Place the Macedonia and gelato in dessert serving dishes and garnish with fresh mint leaves.
Serve immediately.

If there is any fruit remaining, cover it and place it in the refrigerator. The fruit will usually last for one to two days before turning brown and mushy.

CHAPTER 17

SWEETS SECRETS

In Tagliacozzo, one of the residents' best-kept secrets is that the tastiest pastries in town are made by the cloistered nuns at the church high up on a hill. To acquire these sweets, you must participate in a ritual that is both mysterious and fascinating.

First, you must go to the church on the hill and ring the bell. The bell is not an electric one; it is on a rope. When you pull the rope of the bell, a nun will turn a small lazy susan that is on the door so that it opens out to you. You won't be able to see the nun's face because they are cloistered nuns and are not permitted to show their faces. Instead, you will hear a voice speak a short greeting in Italian such as "Si" or the voice may ask if you need help.

You must say, "Dolci," which means "sweets." Then, the voice will ask, "Quanto?" which means "how many." The pastries are sold in multiples of six, so you can ask for six, twelve, twenty-four, or thirty-six. After you have told the doorkeeper the quantity you desire, the voice will tell you the cost. (Remember this conversation is going on through the lazy susan; throughout this entire transaction, you will never see a person, you will deal entirely with a disembodied voice.)

You leave the money on the lazy susan. The nun will take the money. In about five minutes, a cardboard silver tray tied up with a nice little bow will appear on the lazy susan. Your sweets, an assortment from the items that have been baked that day, will be inside this tray. When the perfume of the sweets hits you, you will rush home as fast as you can to open up the package!

The pastries are small finger cakes and elegant little cookies, each one handmade by the nuns. But the best part is the taste; they just melt in your mouth and they are not too sweet or heavy, just light and just right!

If you ever visit the cloistered nuns who make the pastries, be sure you have a good command of the Italian language.

I sent a young American cousin of mine, who was attending a university in Italy for three months, to the convent on the hill to buy some sweets. His appearance was like that of many college students of the time, he had long hair and kept all of his belongings in a backpack. Throughout his travels, he had been living in college dorms. His Italian was improving during his journey, but apparently not enough for the nuns' understanding. When he asked for dolci, he pronounced the word doccia (doe-cha), which means "shower." Even though visitors cannot see the nuns, they must be able to see visitors. For the nuns took in my cousin's somewhat scruffy appearance and assumed he was a homeless youth in need of a shower and a place to stay. In five minutes, the lazy susan was turned, and on it was a brown paper bag with a bar of soap wrapped in plastic, a toothbrush (also wrapped in plastic), and two slices of bread.

So be sure, when dealing with the pastry-making nuns of Tagliacozzo, to pronounce the "i" in dolci (duhl-chee).

BISCOTTI DI FERRARA

Note: Biscotti means "twice baked" and refers to all cookies that are twice baked, like these are. They may come in all different shapes, but, in America, we are used to seeing these shaped in the typical biscotti shape.

15 egg yolks
2 cups sugar
peel of 1 lemon, grated
1¾ cups flour

Beat the egg yolks with the sugar; add the lemon peel and the flour.
Mix until you achieve a thick dough.
Place the dough on a floured wooden board, lightly dust the dough with flour, and form it into a long log.
Cut the log into small pieces. Form the cut pieces into the shape of an "S."

Butter and flour a piece of baking paper and place the S-shaped pieces, or biscotti, on the baking sheet. When placing the biscotti on top of the baking paper, be sure there is distance between each one.

Bake the biscotti at 320 degrees F for 40 minutes or until golden brown.

CANTUCCI BISCOTTI

These are famous all over Italy and are great eaten with Vin Santo, or sweet wine.

2 cups sugar
1 cup almonds, whole and not peeled
4 eggs, beaten
1 tablespoon of grated orange peel
½ teaspoon vanilla flavoring
½ teaspoon baking soda
Butter
Salt

Preheat the oven to 360 degrees F.
Place the almonds on a baking sheet and toast them until they are golden brown.
Then, chop them into large pieces.

Place the flour on a wooden board and make a well.
You will place the following ingredients into the flour well: beaten eggs, baking soda, sugar, and a pinch of salt.
Mix these ingredients with floured hands until the dough is smooth.
Then, add the almonds.

Place a piece of baking paper on top of a baking sheet.
Butter it and then dust it with flour.
Form the pasta into long fingers on the baking sheet.
Bake the long fingers for 15 minutes and, then, remove them from the oven.
Cut the long fingers into slices about ¼-inch thick.
Place the cut slices on a baking sheet and put them back in the oven for 25 minutes.
When they are a golden brown on one side, turn them over and allow them to become a golden color on the other side.

CHAPTER 18
MADONNA DEL PIETRAQUARIA

At the top of a mountain called Monte Salviano, called thus for the salvio, or sage, that grows on it in abundance, is a shrine to the Madonna del Pietraquaria. Every year the townspeople celebrate the feast day of the Madonna and have created a trail up the mountain to the shrine. This path is decorated with the Way of the Cross, different photos depicting the steps that Christ took on His way to Mount Calvary to be crucified. This path is also a popular place to walk, jog, or ride your bike. On Monte Salviano, walking up to the Madonna is, I think, the townspeople's secret for staying thin. I can eat so much when I am there, but as long as I take my weekly or twice-weekly walk to the Madonna, I do not gain any weight. In fact, sometimes I lose weight during my stay there. It is wonderful!

On a Sunday afternoon, you will see many of your neighbors walking up this path that was created by the parks commissioner especially for the summer season. The path is located in a park protected by the Parco d'Abruzzo, the Parks Department of Abruzzo, as a natural reserve. No building is permitted in the park, so when you reach the top of the mountain, the view is spectacular. You can see many of the towns in the surrounding areas as well as the Fucino Valley, which is famous for its potatoes. The Fucino Valley was once a river. The river was filled in and the land was subsidized around the time of World War II for farmers to grow potatoes and vegetables. Some of the land was actually given to farmers free of charge so that they could grow food for their families as well as sell some produce for income.

In August, you can find wild blackberries on Monte Salviano. These blackberries are great for making preserves or marmalade. They also make a delicious topping on gelato or luscious ingredient in a torta, or cake. Everyone watches for these sought-after berries to arrive. So, when you find a spot where the blackberries grow, you must keep an eye on that spot and be quick when it comes time for picking. You can be sure that, on the first Sunday that the blackberries are ripe for picking, they will be gone by 9 a.m. Believe me, I learned this lesson the hard way.

One year, I had everything ready to make my traditional great blackberry marmalade. I had been in Provence and had purchased a sugar that is produced especially for making preserves. You do not need to use as much of this sugar as you would regular sugar. I bought jars and lids. The only thing missing was some fresh Monte Salviano blackberries.

On the Sunday when I knew the blackberries would be ready, we did our weekly jog to the Madonna and, on the way down the mountain, we stopped at the spot where we knew the blackberries were growing. To my surprise, there were no more blackberries! I was crushed. I would have to wait until next August to get my fresh blackberries.

This recipe was given to me by Nicoletta, who runs a charming bed and breakfast in the mountains of Abruzzo and is also a wonderful cook. She is the principal cook there. Most of the bed and breakfast owners in Italy do their own cooking, as well, and usually cook superbly! I had the opportunity to visit Nicoletta and cook with her. Her 'bed and breakfast' (which we call 'agriturismo' in Italian) is located on an organic farm that produces its own wine, hazelnuts, cheeses, breads, fruits, and vegetables.

These biscotti are perfect for a light Italian breakfast of cappuccino and biscotti or mid-morning coffee break, which in Italy would be around 11 a.m. or 12 noon. (Lunch is eaten at about 1-2 p.m.) These cookies also could provide a light sweet conclusion to a meal, accompanying your espresso.

BISCOTTI CON LIMONE

5 eggs
1 cup sugar
1 cup sunflower or peanut oil
3 cups flour
3 teaspoons baking powder
rind of 1 whole lemon (grate only the yellow as the white part of the lemon rind is bitter)
1 teaspoon lemon flavoring

Preheat the oven to 350 degrees F. Line 2 cookie sheet pans with parchment paper.

Place all the ingredients in a mixing bowl in the following order:
First beat the eggs with an electric mixer, then beat in the sugar, a little at a time.
Add the oil and then add the flour, a little at a time.
After half of the flour is added, add in the baking powder, grated lemon rind, and lemon flavoring.
Continue to add the remaining flour a little at a time.
Continue beating the dough with an electric mixer.

Place the dough on the parchment paper, on the cookie sheet, in the form of a long log.
Bake the log for 20 minutes. The log should be a golden color.
Remove the log from the oven and cut it into pieces on an angle to form the biscotti.
The thickness of the biscotti should be your preference.
If they are cut thin, they are lower in calories-however, do not cut them so thin that they break apart.

Place the cut biscotti down on parchment paper on a cookie sheet and place them in an oven at 375 degrees
F for 10 minutes.
Turn the biscotti over and bake for another 10 minutes. The biscotti should be golden brown.

Please note: Oven temperatures do vary, so be careful not to burn the biscotti.
Also, if you prefer a spongy texture to the biscotti, bake them only once.

CHAPTER 19
VIAGGIO IN TRENO

In Italy, no matter how mixed up or illogical things seem, they usually work out in the end. This is never more evident than when dealing with Italy's transportation system. Take the time my brother, who was visiting me, and I decided to meet up with my cousin in Positano, where she was attending a meeting. To get to Positano, my brother and I had to take a train from Avezzano to Rome and then on to Naples. From Naples, we would take the metro train, or subway system, to a little town outside of Sorrento, where we would catch a bus to take us up the winding, narrow, mountainside road to Amalfi and Positano. The views, on this journey, are well worth the logistical nightmare and the death-defying bus ride.

We left Avezzano early on the morning of our journey. We arrived in Rome quite promptly and with no hitches. Perhaps the rest of the trip would go as smoothly, I thought. We proceeded, with tickets in hand, to Track (or binario) 24 to catch the train to Naples. The train was to leave in forty-five minutes, so we thought we had plenty of time to grab something small to munch on, a slice of pizza, a panino, or a small pastry. My stomach started growling at the smell of fresh baked bread wafting from a passing shop.

Our arms were full with luggage and camera bags, so we decided that I would sit on the train with the bags, and John, my brother, would go in search of a snack. (The train was parked, and passengers were coming and going.) After we found seats and got the bags situated nearby, I pulled out a 10,000 lira bill and handed it to John. "Be sure to be back on time; I don't want to go through the train station of Naples alone with these expensive cameras and bags!"

"No problem," John assured me. The trains usually departed a little late, and he figured he would be back within fifteen minutes, well before the train was scheduled to leave.

John had only been gone five minutes when I felt the train start to move. I panicked! Not only was his luggage with me but so was his passport, money, and tickets. How would he get to Positano? And how would I navigate the Naples train station alone, loaded down with all of these bags? Someone was sure to steal our cameras there!

An old man seated in front of me noticed my state of frenzy. When I saw him staring at me, I explained my dilemma. He told me not to worry. The trains always did this, he said. Sometimes, they needed to get out of the way of other trains, and they would move forward for about five minutes, then they would go back to the station.

Still, I was worried about my brother. When he returns to Binario 24, he will think that the train left for Naples without him. And that's exactly what he did think. He went to the ticket window at the train station and was informed that the train should be returning in a few minutes and not to worry. As I said, in Italy, things usually seem to work out in the end. After about ten minutes of moving forward, the train finally moved backward to our starting point. John was waiting there for me and managed to get on the train.

We had a smooth and scenic ride to Naples. The rest of the trip, the subway ride and harrowing mountain bus ride, was uneventful. We arrived in Positano safely and with all our luggage and cameras. I should have known that everything would work out. After all, I'm Italian.

TORTA DI MANDORLE (ALMOND CAKE RECIPE)

1 pound almonds
1/3 cup sugar
1/3 cup milk
8 ounces dark chocolate
1/3 cup butter
6 eggs, separated
¼ cup flour
¼ cup Cointreau liqueur

Place the almonds and the chocolate in a food processor and chop them, finely.
(Do not chop the chocolate into a powder. It should remain in chunks.)

In a separate bowl, beat the egg whites until they are fluffy.
Add in the egg yolks, softened butter, chopped almonds/chocolate mixture, and the flour.
Stir this batter with a wooden spoon.

Butter and flour a cake pan and pour in the batter. Bake at 350 degrees F for 25-30 minutes.

When the cake is cool, dust it with powdered sugar.

Italian Drinks

BEVANDA

Sunday afternoons in Rome are wonderfully relaxing and filled with many pleasures. Just taking an espresso or an aperitivo in one of Rome's most elegant coffee bars can make a whole afternoon. There is nothing like spending leisure Sunday afternoons in the Eternal City.

CHAPTER 20

CALDO, FREDDO & DESSERT
(HOT, COLD & DESSERT)

How can you describe a sunny Sunday afternoon in Rome? It brings to mind the Italian saying of 'e dolce fare niente' (how sweet it is to do nothing). It is an afternoon of doing nothing but in a special way.

One of the great pleasures of Roman life is to sip a coffee or 'aperitivo' at an outdoor café and just watch the world go by. Two of the most scenic spots are Piazza Navona and the Pantheon. Described as the 'theatre of Baroque Rome', Piazza Navona is peopled by street performers and artists peddling their wares, camera-clutching tourists and parents chasing children chasing pigeons.

If you sip your espresso or aperitivo from your café table at the Piazza della Rotonda you can set your gaze at both the majestic Pantheon originally built in 27 BC and rebuilt in 120 AD, as well as the beautiful fountain designed by Giacomo della Porta where ancient Rome meets Renaissance Rome.

The view is worth every penny you pay for that overpriced coffee or aperitivo. When in Rome do like the Romans do and make a Sunday afternoon out of drinking a single espresso or aperitivo.

Who says that food and fashion have nothing in common? In Rome it is fashionably chic to get dressed up in the afternoon for the passeggiata (afternoon walk) and present a 'bella figura' and stroll to the most fashionable coffee bars and sit and sip. Coffees and aperitifs are always served most elegantly.

Aperitivi (aperitifs) are an important part of Italian dining and spark your appetite and stimulate your taste buds. They are usually bitter and do not have a high alcohol content and should have a good balance of bitterness and acidity and without too much sweetness. Alcohol dulls your taste bud. You want to have use of every taste bud. A true Italian meal will be a feast for the senses.

I have always observed that everything in Italy is orchestrated like an opera and the meal is no exception. Starting with the aperitif and appetizer as your overture building up to the first and second courses, then building up to the dessert and espresso and the after dinner drink as your final act.

Caldo
(hot)
BEVANDA

CIOCCOLATA CALDA (HOT CHOCOLATE)

40 grams of semi-sweet or dark chocolate (minimum 70% cocoa). This should be a good quality chocolate with high cocoa content.

1 ½ cups milk
Sugar to taste
Whipped Cream to top

Cut chocolate into small pieces.
Place chocolate in a double boiler pan with 1 tbsp of the milk. When chocolate is melted remove from heat.
With a wooden spoon stir melted chocolate until a soft paste is formed.
In the meantime heat the milk until it is almost boiling be sure to remove from heat just before boiling.
Stir hot milk into melted chocolate mixture (with wooden spoon) and stir in a little at a time
The trick to making a perfect cup of delectable hot chocolate is not to boil the chocolate or it will become bitter.

CIOCCOBIANCO (HOT WHITE CHOCOLATE)

5 tbsps mint liqueur or non-alcoholic mint syrup
1 1/2 cups cream
10 ounces white chocolate
¼ cup sugar
4 mint leaves

Add milk, ½ of cream, sugar in a pan and bring to a boil.
Add finely chopped white chocolate and cook over low heat for 5 minutes.
Add in the liqueur.
Whip remaining cream until peaks form.
Place liquid mixture in 4 cups.
Top with whipped cream and decorate with mint leaves.

CIOCCOCAFE (CHOCOLATE COFFEE)

Makes 4 cups.

1-cup hot black espresso coffee
1/3 cup unsweetened cocoa (use good quality one)
1 1/2 cups milk
1/2-cup sugar
½ tblsp flour
1 cinnamon stick
The peel of 1 orange (be careful not to take any of the white membrane when peeling. Peel off only the orange. The white membrane is bitter)
3/4-cup dl of whipping cream
1 tbsp powdered sugar
2 ounces bittersweet dark chocolate pieces (be sure chocolate has high cocoa content)

Place the milk in a pan with the cinnamon stick and orange peel and heat until just before boiling.
In a bowl mix the sugar, flour, cocoa.
Add hot milk leaving in the cinnamon stick and orange peel.
Mix the milk in a little at a time with wooden spoon.
Place this mix in a pan and place on medium heat.
Mix continually with a wooden spoon for 15 minutes.
Then add in the hot coffee and let cook for another 2 minutes.
Beat chilled whipping cream in a chilled bowl until peaks form.
While whipping, before finished, add powdered sugar and then chocolate chopped finely.

Remove orange peel and cinnamon stick from milk mixture and place in hot chocolate cups.
Top with whipped cream and serve.

CIOCCOPEPPER (HOT CHOCOLATE WITH PEPPER)

8 ounces good quality bittersweet chocolate (should have high cocoa content)
4 ounces milk chocolate (good quality)
1-cup cream
1/2 tsp black or white freshly ground pepper
2 cardamom seeds
1 cinnamon stick
1 tbsp brandy or rum
1/4 tsp almond flavoring
1 tbsp almonds thinly sliced

Bring cream, pepper, cardamom seeds, cinnamon stick to a boil.
Remove from heat and let stand for 15 minutes.
Place mixture through cheesecloth filter and then place filtered mixture in pan and bring to boil again.
Take off heat.
Add in both chocolates finely chopped.
Place on heat for 8 minutes.
Then add in rum and ¼ tsp almond extract.
Divide into 4 cups.
You can top with some freshly ground pepper and almond slices.

CAFFE MOCHA

½ cup honey
1 tbsp unsweetened cocoa powder (use good quality cocoa)
¼ tsp cinnamon
1 1/2 cups hot espresso or dark roast coffee
¾ cup hot milk
¾ cup whipping cream
2 tbsps powdered sugar

Whip the whipping cream with the powdered sugar in a chilled bowl.
Whip until peaks form and then place in the refrigerator.
In another bowl mix the honey with powdered cocoa and cinnamon then let this sit for 5 minutes.
Distribute mixture in 4 cups.
Mix the coffee with milk then place in cups.
Stir and top with whipped cream mix.

ALLA VANIGLIA (WITH VANILLA)

1-cup milk
1 ½ cups cream
1 vanilla stick
¼ tsp cinnamon
Pinch of powdered nutmeg
8 ounces white chocolate

Place milk and cream in a pan.
Add vanilla stick, cinnamon, nutmeg.
Bring to a boil.
Take the pan off of the heat and let stand for 15 minutes.
Filter this mix through cheesecloth.
Place filtered milk in a pan and place in white chocolate chopped finely.
Heat over medium low heat for 5 minutes while mixing with a wooden spoon.
Take the pan off of the heat. (Optional: you can add 4 tbsps of brandy or orange liqueur).
Pour in 4 cups and serve.

CAPPUCCINO EGGNOG

5 medium eggs at room temperature
2 cups milk
½ cup sugar
3 tbsps instant coffee
4 tbsps rum
½ cup cream
½ tsp vanilla
¼ tsp cinnamon

In a bowl beat the eggs with 2 tbsps of milk and powdered coffee.
Place the remaining milk with the sugar, vanilla and cinnamon in the pan.
Heat over low heat until warm.
Stir with a wooden spoon continuously.
Remove from heat.
Add a little at a time to egg mixture.
Whip cream to light peaks in separate bowl.
Transfer this to a pan and cook for 5- 6 minutes continuously stirring with wooden spoon.
Remove from heat and add in rum.
Gently stir in whipped cream and place in 4 cups and serve immediately.

CREMA AL MASCARPONE (CREAM WITH MASCARPONE CHEESE)

2 ½ cups milk
½ cup powdered cocoa (use good quality cocoa)
½ tbsp flour
¼ cup sugar
1 vanilla stick
Peel of ½ orange
8 ounces mascarpone cheese
½ tablespoon cinnamon
1 tbsp powdered sugar
2.5 ounces white chocolate
1 tbsp thinly sliced almonds

Mix in mascarpone with cinnamon, powdered sugar, white chocolate chopped finely in a bowl.

Using a pan, bring the milk to a boil along with the vanilla stick and orange peel.

(You can also place the vanilla stick and orange peel in small cheesecloth sack and when finished just take them out the sack).

Use a bowl and a wooden spoon to mix, cocoa, flour and sugar with a tbsp of milk until mix becomes creamy.

Take out the vanilla stick and orange peel from milk mix and add milk into coca mix a little at a time.

Place this mix in a pan and let cook on medium low heat for 15 minutes mixing continuously with wooden spoon.

Divide cocoa mix into 4 cups.

Fill the cups 2/3 full.

Top each with ¼ of mascarpone cheese.

Sprinkle a few thinly sliced almonds on top for decoration and serve.

SPEZIATO (SPICED)

2 cups milk
2 tbsps flour
1/3-cup sugar
½ cup powdered cocoa (use good quality cocoa)
1 cup filtered orange juice (pulp removed)
4 cloves
1 cinnamon stick
4 tbsps instant coffee powder
For decoration; 4 cinnamon sticks
Orange peel (cut into thin strips)

Place cloves, 1 cinnamon stick and orange juice in pan and bring to boil, then let rest.
Heat milk. Do not boil.
Mix sugar, flour, and powdered coffee, cocoa with a little hot milk in a bowl.
Mix until it becomes creamy.
Add the rest of the milk a little at a time.
Transfer this mix to a pan and heat on low heat for 15 minutes just until boiling.
Add orange juice and cook for another 2 minutes.
Place in 4 cups and decorate with cinnamon stick with a strip of orange peel.

Freddo

BEVANDA

(cold)

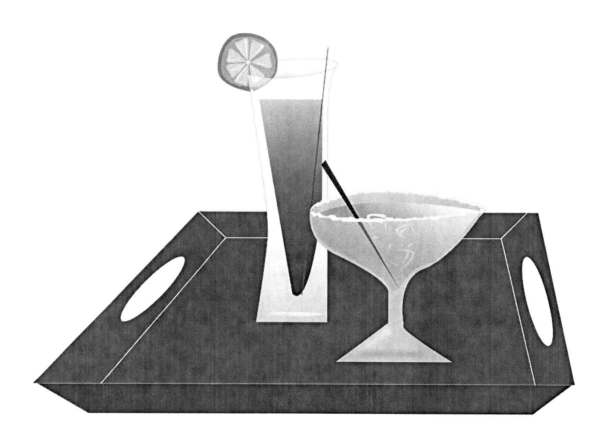

GRANITA AL CAFFE (ITALIAN STYLE ICED COFFEE)

Makes 4 servings

1 ½ cups espresso coffee (use a good quality coffee like Illy)
1 cup of spring water
3 tablespoons of sugar
1 vanilla stick
Crushed ice

Place water, sugar and the vanilla stick in a pan and let boil.
When boiling, take off heat.
Let cool and take out vanilla stick.
Place in an ice cube tray and let this mixture turn to ice in the freezer.
When frozen, place ice in ice crusher to crush or chop with knife (carefully).
Place 3 tbsps of crushed or chopped ice in each glass pour hot coffee (just made) over the ice.
Serve immediately.

SPICED PEAR WINE

Makes 1 carafe

1 bottle of rose wine
2 fresh pears
1 cinnamon stick

Cut cinnamon stick up into small pieces.
Make a small herb sack out of cheesecloth or use an empty teabag and place in the cut cinnamon stick and close the bag.
Set aside.
Peel the pear and cut into small cubes.
Leave a few cubes for decoration.
Fill a carafe with the wine, place in the pear cubes and the sack with the cinnamon stick and let stand in refrigerator for 1 hour.
Filter the wine (taking out pear cubes and cinnamon stick sack.
Pour into individual serving glasses.
Garnish each glass with a cube of pear.
Serve as an aperitif.

MINTED PEAR COCKTAIL (COCKTAIL DI PERA ALLA MENTA)

Makes 4 servings

4 large, tall pears
1 cup of pear juice
Juice of 1 fresh lemon
Fresh mint leaves

Wash pear and cut off the top, about 1/8th inch down.
Hollow out inside of pear with a small spoon.
Place pulp in blender.
Add juice of fresh lemon and pear juice.
Pour this mix in hollowed out pears.
Place some mint leaves on the rim of the pear.
Place a small straw inside and fit top back on.
Serve each individual pear on 1 small serving dish garnished with fresh mint leaves.

HONEY COCKTAIL (COCKTAIL AL MIELE)

Makes 1 carafe

3 cups of white grape juice
Juice of 1 lemon
Honey
Almond milk sweetened
Zest of 1 lemon
A few grapes

Place in the carafe 1 cup of grape juice, lemon juice, 2 tablespoons of honey and 1 cup of almond milk.
Place carafe in refrigerator and chill for two hours.
Peel lemon being careful only to take yellow par of peel.
Cut peel into long thin strips.
When cocktail has chilled place in glasses and decorate with 1 long strip of lemon peel and a toothpick with 2 grapes attached (shish kebab style).
You can serve this with frozen grapes that you make in this way: Place 20 grapes in ice cube tray, cover with some spring water and add a tablespoon of lemon syrup.
Freeze, place cubes in beverage and serve.

POMODORO DRINK (TOMATO DRINK)

Makes 4 servings

1 ¼ cups tomato juice
¼ lb of fresh celery hearts
2 tbsps of onion
1 pound of fresh carrots
Celery leaves for decoration

Chill tomato juice in the refrigerator.
Wash celery hearts.
Dry well.
Attempt to take out any 'threads' of the celery.
Peel onion and chop into small pieces.
Wash, peel and clean carrots, dry and chop into small pieces.
Place all 3 vegetables into juicer.
Transfer the juice, minus the pulp into a tall carafe.
Add in ice cubes and mix well to blend.
Divide the juice into 4 glasses and decorate by placing a short stick of celery with leaves attached into each glass.

ORANGE LIQUEUR (RATAFIA DI ARANCIA)

4 juicing oranges (preferably organic)
1 piece of lemon peel
1 cinnamon stick
1 clove
1 vanilla bean
2-½ cups pure alcohol (for liquor)
¾ cup sugar
½ cup spring, distilled or purified drinking water

Finely grate orange peel; only use the orange part being careful not to take any white membrane, which will make this bitter.
Juice oranges and filter juice through a cheesecloth or gauze.
Place in pitcher with lemon peel, orange peel, alcohol.
Mix with long wooden spoon, cover and let sit for 1 day.
Boil the water and dissolve sugar, let cool.
When cool, place sugar syrup into alcohol mix and let sit for 1 month.
Be sure it is in a tightly closed bottle you will have to shake the bottle to mix every few days.
After 1 month, filter liquor through cheesecloth or gauze.
Place in liquor bottle and let stay for another month.
Then serve.

ORANGE FLAVORED CAMPARI (CAMPARI ALL ARANCIA)

Makes 1 serving

3 tbsps Campari liqueur
1 thick lemon slice
3 ice cubes
1/3 cup orange juice

In a small glass place 3 tblsps Campari liqueur, 13 cup orange juice, ice cubes and top with a thick slice of fresh orange. Serve

AROMATIC ROSÉ WINE (VINO ROSE AROMATICA)

1 liter rose wine
1 orange peeled and sliced
1 lemon peeled and sliced
2 tbsps sugar
5 mint leaves

Place all ingredients in wine carafe except mint leaves.
Stir and serve in individual glasses.
Use mint leaves for decorations in serving glasses.

PORTOFINO

(Before dinner aperitif)

1/3-cup fresh strawberries
1/3-cup fresh peach juice
1/3-cup fresh orange juice

Put all ingredients in blender for 5 seconds.
Serve with crushed ice and garnish with 2 peach slices and a whole strawberry.

KIWI APERITIVE (APERITIVO DI KIWI)

¼ cup spring or distilled or purified drinking water
¼ cup sugar
A pinch of powdered ginger
3 kiwi-peeled and cut in quarters
2 tablespoons of crushed ice
¼ cup fresh lemon juice

Place in pan water, sugar and pinch of ginger.
Let come to a boil, remove from heat.
Place kiwi, ice, lemon juice and cooled syrup in a blender.
Blend for 2 minutes.
Serve immediately.

MANDARIN APERITIVE (APERITIVO AL MANDARINO)

3 pounds of mandarin oranges
1 ½ cups Martini (White and dry)
8 tbsps bitter Campari soda
1 orange
Ice cubes
2 tbsps sugar

Juice Mandarins.
Filter juice through gauze or cheesecloth.
Place in carafe and chill in refrigerator for 1 hour.
Then add in martini, Campari, sugar and 3 ice cubes.
Stir with long wooden spoon.

Wash and dry orange.
With lemon peeler, peel 8 long spiral pieces of peel from orange for decoration.
Pour aperitive into 8 glasses and decorate with orange spirals and some ice cubes.

ITALIAN STYLE MIMOSA (MIMOSA ITALIANA)

1/2 cup Prosecco Spumante (Italian champagne)
¼ cup orange juice (preferably fresh)

Squeeze orange juice, place into a long champagne flute.
Stir gently to avoid too much foam.

ITALIAN STYLE SANGRIA

1 bottle of red wine (preferably Montepulciano or Chianti)
2 cups sparkling water
½ cup Cognac
1 cinnamon stick
2 tbsps sugar
1 orange
1 lemon
2 fresh peaches
4 ounces strawberries
4 ounces raspberries
Orange peel
Cloves
2 tbsps raspberry syrup

Cut fruit and place in large wine carafe with all ingredients except sparkling water.
Let sit for 2 hours, and then add sparkling water and serve.

TINTORETTO

½ cup Prosecco Spumante
¼ cup pomegranate juice

Place prosecco into champagne flute, top with pomegranate juice.
Stir gently to avoid too much foam.
Garnish with a few pomegranate seeds and a whole strawberry.

LIMONCELLO

In Italy it is you cannot call this drink Limoncello unless you use the large sweet lemons of Sorrento (which are as sweet as candy and grown without pesticides). There is a trademark on the formula used to make this. However, you can attempt to make something similar here. Try to use fresh if possible organic lemons to get the best quality.

3 organic fresh lemons
2-½ cups pure alcohol for liquors
1 leaf of Melissa
¼ cup sugar
2 cups of spring, distilled or purified drinking water

Wash the lemons, dry and grate the peels, be careful to only take the yellow part of the peel and not the white membrane, which is bitter..
Place in a liquor bottle with alcohol and let sit for 7 days.
Shake bottle every so often.
Heat water, let sugar dissolve in heated water, be careful not to boil.
Remove from heat once sugar is dissolved and let this mixture cool.
Juice 2 lemons.
When syrup has cooled, mix into alcohol mixture with lemon juice.
Let mixture stand for another 7 days.
Filter this mixture and bottle in liquor bottle with cork or top.
Let stand for at least 2 months.
You can store Limoncello in the freezer. Because of its high alcohol content it will not freeze it will only become very cold and add to the refreshing characteristic of this liquor.
This can be used as an after dinner drink or poured over crushed ice for a granite di limoncello.

ITALIAN SODA

4 bottles (about 12 ounces each) of assorted flavored syrup
(Use the flavored syrups fro your favorite coffee bars. Choose any flavors that you prefer.)
8 bottles of sparkling water (about 1 quart each)
1 lime sliced
1 lemon sliced
½ cup fresh strawberries
2 fresh peaches sliced
Fresh raspberries
Crushed ice

Fill ten tall glasses with crushed ice.
Add 3 tbsps of flavored syrup to each glass. (Pour it onto the ice already in the glass).
Fill glasses with sparkling water.
Garnish each glass with fresh fruit slices of your choice and serve.

SPICY ICED TEA (TE FREDDO PROFUMATO ALLA SPEZIE)

2 tbsps of black tea leaves (Darjeeling tea is best for this recipe but you can try other black teas).
1 vanilla stick
1 cup of maple syrup
1 quart of spring water
1 star of anise fruit

Heat 1 liter of spring water in a pan.
Right before water begins to boil, add tea leaves loose or place leaves in tea ball and add in to water.
Immediately remove from heat and after 5 minutes remove tealeaves.
Cut vanilla stick in half lengthwise and add into hot tea.
Place in heat resistant pitcher, cover and let cool in refrigerator.
Cut start of anise fruit into 4-5 pieces, place into maple syrup in another container.
Let sit until tea has cooled.
When ready to serve cooled tea, remove star of anise fruit from syrup.
Place tea in glasses and add in syrup to sweeten.

LEMON SYRUP

3 fresh ripe lemons
1-cup water
3 cups sugar

Peel lemons carefully by taking off the yellow part of the peel only.
Do not include the white part of the peel or it will make the syrup bitter.
Put peeled lemon aside.

Cut yellow lemon peel into thin strips.
Place water in saucepan and heat till hot, but not boiling.
Place heat on low, or just warm enough to simmer.
Place in lemon peel. After 3 minutes, take out the lemon zest.
Stir in 3 cups of sugar and the inside of the lemon or lemon pulp (already seeded).
Simmer this mixture over low heat stirring constantly with a wooden spoon until syrup has the consistency of oil and looks similar to white wine.
When cool use for the recipe for Italian soda or to top vanilla ice cream.
Store syrup in glass jar when cooled.

CINNAMON SYRUP (SCIROPPO DI CANELLA)

1 pound of sugar
2 ½ cups spring or distilled water or purified drinking water.
2 cinnamon sticks

Place in casserole the sugar with water.
Place over heat and let boil for 10 minutes stirring slowly with spoon.
When boiling add in cinnamon sticks and cook for 2 minutes more.
Let cool and then filter.
Place in glass bottle and refrigerate.
Will keep up to 1 month in refrigerator.

GINGER SYRUP

1-pound sugar
2 ½ cups spring water
1- 5 inch ginger root- peeled and cut into small sticks

Place the sugar, water and ginger root into a pan.
Place over low heat and stir with wooden spoon.
When sugar has melted into mixture, raise the heat to medium low and bring to a boil.
Boil for 10 minutes consistently stirring slowly with a wooden spoon.
Remove from heat.
Let cool.
When cooled, filter the mixture.
This will keep in the refrigerator in an enclosed container for up to 1 month.

(Note- if you would like to make saffron syrup you can substitute 1 small envelope of saffron for the ginger.
Yellow saffron, which is well known in Abruzzo, works well with this.

WITH CREAM (ALLA CREMA)

1-cup water
6 tsps instant coffee
3 tsps sugar
1 tbsp of coffee liqueur
2 ice cubes
Whipped cream

In a shaker place water, coffee, sugar, coffee liqueur, ice cubes.
Shake vigorously. Pour into tall glass.
Place whipped cream on top.
Add whipped cream by spoon, letting the cream fall down the spoon.
Sprinkle powdered cocoa on top.
Serve immediately

Dessert

BEVANDA

FRULLATTO AL CAFFE (COFFEE FRULLATO OR MILKSHAKE)

2 cups of strong espresso coffee
4 tbsps of sugar
2 cups of chopped ice
1 tsp of anisette or amaretto liqueur

Put all of the ingredients in a blender and blend for 30 seconds.
Serve immediately in two tall chilled glasses.

RASPBERRY FRULLATO (FRULLATO AL LAMPONI)

Makes 4 servings

1 pound of fresh raspberries
3 white peaches
3 tbsps of lemon juice
2 tbsps of cinnamon syrup
¾ cup orange juice (preferably blood red orange juice)

Place on 4 toothpicks each, 4 washed raspberries and one small piece of washed white peach. Set aside.
Place in blender the remainder of raspberries that have been carefully washed, the peaches that remain that have been washed and peeled, lemon juice, 1/3 cup orange juice, cinnamon syrup (see recipe below).
Place mixture in aluminum container and place in freezer for 40 minutes.
Do not totally freeze.
Pour into 4 large glasses, and add in the rest of the orange juice divided equally into 4 glasses. Complete by topping with the fruit on the toothpick.
Serve immediately.

BANANA ALMOND FRULLATO (BANANA MANDORLE FRULLATO)

Makes 4 servings

4 bananas
¾ cup filtered fresh lemon juice
1 2/3 cup of whole milk plain yogurt
1 cup of almond flavored syrup
Chopped ice

Peel and slice the banana.
Set aside 8 slices for decoration and splash some lemon juice on them to keep from becoming brown.
Place the bananas in the blender with remaining lemon juice.
Add in almond syrup and yogurt and blend for another 20 seconds.
Divide the frullato into 4 glasses and add in some chopped ice and serve.
Decorate each glass with 2 banana slices on a toothpick.

FRULLATO DI FRAGOLE E BANANA
(FRULLATO WITH STRAWBERRIES AND BANANA)

Makes 4 servings

1-cup whole (or 2%) milk
4 ounces whole milk plain yogurt
1 banana
¼ lb strawberries
1 tbsp honey
4 ice cubes

Wash and hull the strawberries.
Carefully dry strawberries with towel paper.
Set aside 4 whole strawberries for decoration. (Only wash the 4 strawberries for decoration–do not hull.)
Peel banana.
Slice banana, put aside 4 slices for decoration.

Chill 4 empty glasses (approx 8oz glasses) in refrigerator for 10 minutes.
Place milk, yogurt, bananas, strawberries, honey and 4 ice cubes in a blender.
Blend for 2 minutes or until a creamy texture is obtained.
Don't blend too long or mix will become watery.

Take glasses out of the refrigerator.
Immediately divide mix into 4 glasses. On the rim of each glass, cut a slice of banana half way into glass so it hangs on rim.
Do the same with whole strawberry.
Serve.

MANGO FRULLATO

Makes 4 servings

2 mangoes
2 papayas
4 tblsps of fresh lemon juice
4 tblsps lemon syrup
2 tbsps sugar
1 tbsp cinnamon
1 cup unsweetened pineapple juice (fresh if possible)

Sprinkle some of the lemon juice along the rims of glasses to wet them.
Mix sugar with cinnamon, sprinkle on top of rim already wet with lemon juice so it will stick.
Remove skin from papaya and take out seeds.
Remove skin and pit from mango.
Cut the fruit into small pieces.
Set aside 2 slices of mango for decoration.
Place the rest of the mango and papaya in blender with juice of 1 lemon and lemon syrup.
Divide the juice into the 4 serving glasses.
Cut both slices of mango set aside into 4 small pieces.
Arrange on toothpick 2 pieces of each slice, one piece on top of the other.
Place in glass for decoration.
Place in some crushed ice if you like.

BERRY FRULLATO (FRULLATO DI MORE E MIRTILLI)

Makes 4 serrvings

1-cup blueberries
¾ cup blackberries
Juice of 3 limes (preferably fresh)
10 fresh mint leaves
4 tbsps sugar
16 ounces of sparkling water or plain club soda
30 small ice cubes

Carefully wash the blueberries and the blackberries.
Place in blender with limejuice.
Divide the frullato into 4 glasses and chill in the refrigerator.
Finely chop mint leaves.
Take 2 sheets of baking paper.
Lay chopped mint leaves in one layer on one baking paper sheet.
Sprinkle with sugar.
Cover with other sheet of baking paper.
GO overtop layer with meat tenderizer tool.
Crush ice in ice crusher or with ice pick.
Place mint leaf/sugar mixture in a small bowl and then mix in crushed ice.
Take out chilled glasses with fruit juice from refrigerator and place in ice cubes.
Complete with sparkling water or club soda.
Pour 4 ounces of the soda into each glass.
Serve immediately.

KIWI APPLE FRULLATO (FRULLATO DI KIWI E MELA)

4 kiwis
1 cup of apple juice (preferably granny smith apple juice)
½ cup ginger flavored syrup
½ cup fresh lemon juice filtered
Chopped ice

Peel 3 kiwi and cut into pieces.
Place in blender with lemon juice and 2 tablespoons of crushed ice and blend for 2 minutes.
Add in ginger flavored syrup and blend for another 15 seconds.
Divide the mix equally into 4 glasses.
Then add into each glass ¼ cup apple juice.
Add in some crushed ice to taste if you like.
Peel and cut 4th kiwi into 8 slices place two into each drink or hang on rim of glass.

FRAGOLE FRAPPE (STRAWBERRY FRAPPE)

Makes 10 servings

2 quarts of milk
1 pound of frozen strawberries
3 tbsps of sugar
10 fresh strawberries

Place the milk and frozen strawberries in the blender (by using frozen strawberries instead of fresh you can avoid adding ice cubes and hence this will not be watery but creamy), also add in the sugar.
Blend on high until the mix is well blended, thick and creamy.
Should be of a whipped consistency.
Be careful not to beat too long or it will be come watery.
Time of blending varies depending on power of blender.
Pour frappe into 10 small serving glasses.
Garnish each glass with colored straw and a whole strawberry pressed down onto rim of glass so that strawberry will hang on rim.

SPICY DESSERT COFFEE (CAFFE DOLCE E SPEZIATA)

This makes a great after dinner drink, especially in the winter.

2 cups boiling hot espresso coffee
2 tsps sugar
½ cup dark rum (heated)
4 tbsps whipped cream
Pinch of nutmeg
Pinch of cinnamon

Warm rum. (Do not boil).
Place boiling hot coffee in heat resistant pitcher.
Add in heated rum, sugar and stir with long wooden spoon.
Pour into 2 glass espresso cups, top with whipped cream and dust with nutmeg and cinnamon.

LEMON SORBETTO

This refreshing mixture can be served as a beverage or a dessert.

5 fresh lemons
2 cups of spring, distilled or purified drinking water
½ cup sugar
1 cup Port wine
½ cup whipping cream
Fresh mint leaves

Juice lemons and filter the juice.
Place filtered lemon juice, water, sugar and Port wine in a blender.
Blend until sugar is dissolved.
Whip cream and fold gently into mixture with spatula.
Place mixture is flat ice cube tray or aluminum pan and leave in freezer for 1 hour.
Take out of freezer and stir with spatula to form a smooth 'slush'.
Return to freezer for another hour.
Then place in blender.
Return to tray and leave in freezer for 1 hour then serve.
Garnish with fresh mint leaves on top.

CHOCOLATE LIQUEUR

2 cups milk
2 cups sugar
1/3 cup unsweetened cocoa powder (use good quality cocoa)
1/3-cup pure alcohol

Place sugar, powdered cocoa in pan; add in milk, stirring in a little at a time.
Stir continuously to avoid lumps forming.

Once mixture is well blended, place on heat and let boil at medium heat for 20 minutes.
Keep stirring continuously with wooden spoon.

Remove from heat.
When mixture has cooled, add in alcohol.
Place in liqueur bottle and shake well before serving.

Menu Suggestions...

Romantic Dinner for Two

Cocktail: TINTORETTO

½ cup Prosecco Spumante
¼ cup pomegranate juice
Place prosecco into champagne flute, top with pomegranate juice.
Stir gently to avoid too much foam.
Garnish with a few pomegranate seeds and a whole strawberry.

Appetizer: BRUSCHETTA GRATINATE

To make bruschetta, you must first get crusty Italian bread.
¼ pound fontina cheese
3 leaves of arugula
2 very ripe tomatoes
5 slices of crusty bread
1 tablespoon olive oil

Cut the fontina cheese into small slices.
Then, cut the tomatoes into very tiny cubes, eliminating the seeds.
Chop the arugula finely.

Put the bruschetta bread in the oven for about 5 minutes and let it brown and harden slightly.
Then, remove the bread from the oven.

Place cheese slices on top of the bread. Sprinkle with chopped arugula.
Place the tomatoes on top and place the bruschetta in the oven until the cheese starts to melt.
Take the bruschetta out of the oven and serve it immediately.

First Course: LINGUINE ALLE VONGOLE (CLAMS WITH LINGUINE)

1 pound linguine
4 tablespoons olive oil
3-4 cloves garlic
1 pound fresh steamed clams
1 tablespoon parsley
½ lemon (to squeeze over pasta when finished)

Begin boiling water for the pasta before making the clam sauce.

Sauté crushed or whole garlic in a pan until it starts to become golden-about three minutes. Add the clams and sauté for 5 minutes, add chopped parsley and sauté for about one minute. Remove from fire.

Boil water for the pasta in a large, tall pasta pot.
Put the linguine in the boiling water
Follow the cooking directions on the side of the package for al dente pasta.
Drain the pasta and place it in the pan to sauté with the clam sauce.
Turn gently with a "pasta pincer" until the pasta is coated with sauce.
Squeeze the ½ lemon over the pasta and turn gently to coat the pasta.

Serve.

Suggested white wines to serve with the first course:

Trebbiano D'Abruzzo
Est!Est!Est

Second Course: PEPPERONI IMBOTTITI (STUFFED PEPPERS)

1½ cups cannelloni beans
½ cup white onion, minced
2 teaspoons fresh garlic, minced finely
½ cup extra virgin cold pressed olive oil
1 can (6 ounces) tuna packed in olive oil
juice from 1 fresh lemon squeezed
1/3 cup freshly chopped parsley
8 fresh peppers
(to make this dish colorful, you can choose an assortment of colors for the peppers, if they are in season)

If you are using dried beans you must first soak them overnight-or for at least 12 hours-covered with water.
Then, drain them and place them in a pot.
Cover them with cold water and cook them for approximately 30 minutes or until they are tender.

Once the beans are cooked, drain them.
Place, in a large bowl, the beans, olive oil, garlic, onions, lemon juice, and salt to taste.

Take the whole peppers; cut off their tops and put them aside.
Scoop out the inside of the peppers and take out the seeds and pulp.
To get the peppers to stand, you can cut off a little piece from the bottom so they sit on a flat surface and can remain upright.

Stuff the peppers with the bean mixture you made.

You can serve these peppers raw as an antipasto or a light meal.
Serve them at home or take them to the beach, in the summertime, as a light lunch.

Dessert: FRESH STRAWBERRIES WITH LEMON (FRAGOLE CON LIMONE)

1 pound fresh strawberries
1 lemon (grown organically)
3 tablespoons sugar (to your taste)
A handful of fresh mint leaves

Wash the strawberries and hull them with a small knife.
If you are using the baby strawberries, or fragolini, you do not have to cut them.
If you are using the normal-sized strawberries, cut each strawberry in half. Squeeze your lemon over the halved strawberries and sprinkle on the sugar.
Refrigerate for one hour and then taste the strawberries after all the flavors have had a chance to marinade.
If you desire a sweeter taste, sprinkle with a touch of sugar.

Divide the strawberries into 4-5 dessert cups, garnish them with mint leaves, and serve them cold, right from the refrigerator.

Serve dessert with a great sparkling wine:

Spumante

After Dinner Drink: CAFFE ALL ARANCIA (ORANGE FLAVORED COFFEE)

4 juicing oranges (preferably organic)
1 piece of lemon peel
1 cinnamon stick
1 clove
1 vanilla bean
2-½ cups pure alcohol (for liquor)
¾ cup sugar
½ cup spring, distilled or purified drinking water

Finely grate orange peel; only use the orange part being careful not to take any white membrane, which will make this bitter.

Juice oranges and filter juice through a cheesecloth or gauze.

Place in pitcher with lemon peel, orange peel, alcohol.

Mix with long wooden spoon, cover and let sit for 1 day.

Boil the water and dissolve sugar, let cool.

When cool, place sugar syrup into alcohol mix and let sit for 1 month.

Be sure it is in a tightly closed bottle you will have to shake the bottle to mix every few days.

After 1 month, filter liquor through cheesecloth or gauze.

Place in liquor bottle and let stay for another month.

Then serve.

Christmas Family Dinner

Aperitifs

FOR THE KIDS: KIWI APERITIF

¼ cup spring or distilled or purified drinking water
¼ cup sugar
A pinch of powdered ginger
3 kiwi-peeled and cut in quarters
2 tablespoons of crushed ice
¼ cup fresh lemon juice

Place in pan water, sugar and pinch of ginger.
Let come to a boil, remove from heat.
Place kiwi, ice, lemon juice and cooled syrup in a blender.
Blend for 2 minutes.
Serve immediately.

FOR THE ADULTS: ITALIAN MIMOSA

1/2 cup Prosecco Spumante (Italian champagne)
¼ cup orange juice (preferably fresh)

Squeeze orange juice, place into a long champagne flute.

Stir gently to avoid too much foam.

Appetizer: CORNETTI DI PROSCIUTTO CON NOCE (HAM WITH NUTS)

4 slices of prosciutto ham
4 ounces of cream cheese
3 ounces of shelled walnuts
a handful of parsley leaves

Set aside 4 whole walnuts and grind, or finely chop, the rest.
Place the cream cheese in a bowl and, with a wooden spoon, mix in the ground nuts. Mix well.
Add about 1 teaspoon of finely chopped parsley leaves. Mix well.
Divide the mixture between 4 slices of prosciutto ham and spread the mixture onto each slice.
Shape each slice of prosciutto into a cone, or horn.
At the opening of each horn, place a whole walnut.
Place all four slices on a serving plate and garnish with parsley leaves.

First course: ITALIAN WEDDING SOUP WITH CROSTINI PER ZUPPA

12 eggs
12 tablespoons flour
12 tablespoons Parmigiana cheese or grated cheese
¼ pound Italian ham (optional)
1 small ball mozzarella cheese (cut into chunks)
2 tablespoons parsley (dried or fresh)
2 tablespoons olive oil

Pour all the ingredients into a bowl.
Grease a cookie sheet with olive oil.
Pour the frittata mixture into the sheet and bake it in the oven at 350 degrees F for 15 minutes.
Then, remove it from the oven.
Let it cool and cut it into small squares, crouton size.
Use this to top stracciatella, Italian wedding soup, and many other soups as well.

Suggested red wines:

Montepulciano di Abruzzo
Chianti

Second Course: LASAGNE BOLOGNESE

For the sauce:
½ onion chopped finely
1 carrot chopped finely
1 stalk of celery chopped finely
2 tablespoons butter
½ pound ground beef
1/3 pound ground pork
¼ pound ground veal
1 cup of tomato sauce
salt and pepper to taste

For the lasagna:
1 pound white flour
2 eggs
½ pound spinach
béchamel sauce (recipe in Part IV)
Butter
Grated Parmigiana-reggiano cheese

Fry the vegetables in butter, add the meat, and brown for a few minutes.
Then add the plain tomato sauce, salt and pepper to taste.
Prepare the pasta by mixing the flour, eggs, and spinach.
(The spinach should be freshly cooked, dried, and passed through a potato masher or food processor.)
Mix all ingredients and roll the dough out on a floured board.
Cut the dough into large rectangular squares, dust with semolina flour, and let it stand.

Butter a large lasagna pan. On the bottom, put a small amount of sauce and grated cheese
Then top this with a layer of lasagna.
Cover this layer of lasagna with more sauce, cheese, and, also, béchamel sauce
Then repeat with another layer of lasagna.
The final layer should be topped with bechamel sauce and a pat of butter.

Bake the lasagna in the oven at 320 degress F for approximately 30 minutes or until the top becomes slightly golden.

For a variation, this can be made without the meat and just with vegetables.

Third Course: PATATE PER FESTE

1 pound potatoes
1 small onion
salt to taste
2 tablespoons butter

Place the potatoes in a large saucepan and add water over them until they are covered with water.
Add in a pinch of gross salt.
Boil the potatoes until they are tender.
Drain and cool the potatoes.

Mash the potatoes.
Finely chop the onions and add them to the potatoes.
Season with salt to taste, add butter and mix.
Place the mixture into small muffin cups.
Place some rosemary or parsley on top.

Bake at 425 degrees F for 35-40 minutes.
Remove the potatoes from the muffin cups and serve.

Dessert: PANETTONE BREAD PUDDING

Fresh fruit Macedonia (made with fresh fruits in season)

2 cups milk
2 eggs
½ teaspoon vanilla
½ cup sugar
Dried panettone cubes (if the panettone is not dried, place it in an oven or toaster for a few minutes)

Blend all the liquid ingredients together.
Arrange panettone cubes in the bottom of a glass pan.
Pour the liquid mixture over the panettone and bake at 350 degrees F for 30 minutes.

Sprinkle baked bread pudding with powdered sugar, or brown sugar, on top.
This can also be served with vanilla ice cream, whip cream, et cetera.

Serve desserts with sparkling wines such as:

Braccheto d'Asti
Spumante

After dinner dessert drinks:

CHOCOLATE LIQUEUR

2 cups milk
2 cups sugar
1/3 cup unsweetened cocoa powder (use good quality cocoa)
1/3-cup pure alcohol

Place sugar, powdered cocoa in pan; add in milk, stirring in a little at a time.
Stir continuously to avoid lumps forming.

Once mixture is well blended, place on heat and let boil at medium heat for 20 minutes.
Keep stirring continuously with wooden spoon.

Remove from heat.
When mixture has cooled, add in alcohol.
Place in liqueur bottle and shake well before serving.

ESPRESSO

Use a quality brand of espresso.

New Years Eve

Aperitif: SPICED PEAR WINE

Makes 1 carafe

1 bottle of rose wine
2 fresh pears
1 cinnamon stick

Cut cinnamon stick up into small pieces.
Make a small herb sack out of cheesecloth or use an empty teabag and place in the cut cinnamon stick and close the bag and set aside.
Peel the pear and cut into small cubes.
Leave a few cubes for decoration.
Fill a carafe with the wine, place in the pear cubes and the sack with the cinnamon stick and let stand in the refrigerator for 1 hour.
Filter the wine (taking out pear cubes and cinnamon stick sack.
Pour into individual serving glasses.
Garnish each glass with a cube of pear.
Serve as an aperitif.

Appetizer: MINTED PEARS WITH PARMIGIANO-REGGIANO CHEESE

2 large Bartlett or bosc pears; these should be ripe but firm
1 slice parmigiano-reggiano cheese
8 slices fresh mint
Balsamic vinegar

Wash and peel the pears.
Slice each pear into 6 slices, eliminating the seeds and core near the seeds.
Crumble the parmigiano reggiano cheese into small chunks.
Take 4 small serving dishes.
On one side of each dish, layer 3 slices of pear with a slice of mint in between each slice.
On the other side of the dish, arrange 3 or 4 small chunks of parmigiano reggiano cheese and sprinkle a small drop of balsamic vinegar on top of the cheese.
Do not saturate the cheese with the vinegar, just slightly wet it to give the cheese a hint of flavor of the balsamic.

First Course: ZUPPA DI LENTICCHIE WITH CROSTINI PER ZUPPA

2 cups dried lentils
3-4 tablespoons olive oil
2 garlic cloves
2 slices of onions
3-4 cups vegetable broth
2 carrots, sliced (optional)
2 potatoes (optional)
1 stick celery, sliced

Soak the lentils in a large bowl of water the night before-or at least 8 hours before-cooking this recipe.
Place oil with garlic cloves and onion slices in a deep saucepan or a large pot.
Heat just until the onions start to become golden.
Pre-cook the potatoes for 3-5 minutes in a pot of boiling water.
In a saucepan, mix lentils with some broth, potatoes, carrots, and celery.
Add more broth as needed.
When the lentils are tender, the soup is done; approximately 20-30 minutes.
Serve hot with home made crostini, or croutons (see next page).

CROSTINI PER ZUPPA

12 eggs
12 tablespoons flour
12 tablespoons Parmigiana cheese or grated cheese
¼ pound Italian ham (optional)
1 small ball mozzarella cheese (cut into chunks)
2 tablespoons parsley (dried or fresh)
2 tablespoons olive oil

Pour all the ingredients into a bowl.
Grease a cookie sheet with olive oil.
Pour the frittata mixture into the sheet and bake it in the oven at 350 degrees F for 15 minutes.
Then, remove it from the oven.
Let it cool and cut it into small squares, crouton size.
Use this to top stracciatella, Italian wedding soup, and many other soups as well.

Second Course: BRACIOLE TOSCANA

4 thin slices of pork used for braciole, or fast fry steaks.
(These should be 1/3 pound each, no bones and thinly cut slices.)
1 clove garlic
a dash of anise seeds, crushed
1 glass of Chianti red wine
Salt and pepper to taste

Salt and pepper the 4 slices of pork.
Place them in a non-stick frying pan with a clove of crushed garlic and anise seeds, crushed as well.
Let the meat become golden; then add the wine.
Cover the pan and continue cooking the meat on low heat until the wine is almost totally burned off.

Serve hot.

Side dish: SPINACI FIORENTINA

2 pounds fresh spinach
4 eggs
4 ounces butter
2½ cups milk
Grated Parmigiana cheese
Flour salt and pepper to taste

Clean the spinach and cook it for about 10 minutes.
Drain it and remove all the water.
Chop it finely and place it in a casserole with half of the butter and a little salt.

In another pan, prepare a béchamel sauce-see Part IV in this book,
For the béchamel recipe-with the rest of the butter, milk, and 2 tablespoons of grated cheese.

Place the spinach in a glass pan that has been buttered.
With a small spoon, make 4 small holes in the spinach in the pan and, in each hole, place a whole egg.
Salt and pepper the egg and cover it with the béchamel sauce.
Place the grated cheese on top and bake in the oven at 360 degrees F for about 20 minutes.

Desserts: TORTA DI MANDORLE

1 pound almonds
1/3 cup sugar
1/3 cup milk
8 ounces dark chocolate
1/3 cup butter
6 eggs, separated
¼ cup flour
¼ cup Cointreau liqueur

Place the almonds and the chocolate in a food processor and chop them, finely.
(Do not chop the chocolate into a powder. It should remain in chunks.)
In a separate bowl, beat the egg whites until they are fluffy.
Add in the egg yolks, softened butter, chopped almonds/chocolate mixture, and the flour.
Stir this batter with a wooden spoon.
Butter and flour a cake pan and pour in the batter. Bake at 350 degrees F for 25-30 minutes.
When the cake is cool, dust it with powdered sugar.

PLATE OF FRESH FRUITS AND NUTS

After Dinner Drink: SPICY DESSERT COFFEE

This makes a great after dinner drink, especially in the winter.

2 cups boiling hot espresso coffee
2 tsps sugar
½ cup dark rum (heated)
4 tbsps whipped cream
Pinch of nutmeg
Pinch of cinnamon

Warm rum. (Do not boil).
Place boiling hot coffee in heat resistant pitcher.
Add in heated rum, sugar and stir with long wooden spoon.
Pour into 2 glass espresso cups, top with whipped cream and dust with nutmeg and cinnamon.

Spring Holiday Menu

Appetizer: TOMATOES WITH BASIL

1 cup breadcrumbs
1 8-ounce can tuna packed in olive oil
1 tablespoon capers
6 small, round, firm tomatoes
1 lemon
fresh Italian parsley
fresh basil

Cut the off tops of the tomatoes and save these tops for later.
Gently remove the seeds and pulp.
Sprinkle a slight pinch of salt over each of the tomatoes to dry them out the inside.
Then, place the tomatoes upside down on absorbent paper towel and let them dry out for about 30 minutes.
Place, in a bowl, the breadcrumbs with tuna and the olive oil.
Mix thoroughly by hand.
Then, add a handful of chopped parsley and the capers with the grated peel of one lemon.
Mix by hand again.
Then, add the juice of one lemon.
Filter the seeds and pulp from the juice.
Mix all ingredients again, by hand, until they are well blended.

Divide the mixture evenly and place some in each tomato.
Place the tops back on the tomatoes and garnish with fresh basil leaves.
You can also drizzle a little olive oil on top when serving.

Suggested red wine for Appetizer:

Chianti
Montepulciano d'Abruzzo

First Course: TORTE SALATE

1 pound small zucchini
3 fresh small onions cut into very thin slices
½ clove garlic crushed
½ cup of water and ½ cup milk, mixed together
4 tablespoons flour
2 eggs
4 tablespoons grated parmigiano cheese
Extra virgin oil
Salt and pepper to taste

Cut the zucchini into thin slices, sprinkle it lightly with salt, and let it stand for 20 minutes.

Then, beat the eggs with the flour and the water-and-milk mixture until the dough is smoothly mixed.

Rinse the zucchini to take out the salt and dry it with a paper towel.
Add the zucchini, onions, grated cheese, and garlic to the dough.

Butter a pie pan and place the zucchini dough mixture in it.
Drizzle it with some olive oil and bake it at 400 degrees F until golden.
Serve warm covered with grated cheese.

Suggested white wines for first and second courses:

Falenghina
Trebbiano d"Abruzzo

Second Course: RISOTTO CON PARMIGIANO

400 grams carnaroli or Arborio rice
1 small onion chopped finely
4 ounces Parmigiana-reggiano cheese, grated
5 ounces butter
4 tablespoons extra virgin olive oil
1 cup broth-chicken or vegetable
1 glass dry white wine
Salt to taste

In a large frying pan, combine the olive oil, broth, and 50 grams of butter.
Sauté the onion in this mixture.
When the onion is golden, add the rice and allow it to become a golden color.
Add the white wine a little at a time and the broth a little at a time.
Stir, all the while keeping the stove on low heat. You should cook the mixture for 15 minutes.
When the rice is "al dente," add the rest of the butter and half of the grated cheese.
Continue to stir.

Place in individual serving dishes and sprinkle with the remaining cheese.
Serve hot.

Dessert: CANTUCCI BISCOTTI SERVED WITH VIN SANTO

These are famous all over Italy and are great eaten with Vin Santo, or sweet wine. They are also sold in a package with this wine, but they are best when baked fresh.

2 cups sugar
1 cup almonds, whole and not peeled
4 eggs, beaten
1 tablespoon of grated orange peel
½ teaspoon vanilla flavoring
½ teaspoon baking soda
Butter
Salt

Preheat the oven to 360 degrees F.
Place the almonds on a baking sheet and toast them until they are golden brown.
Then, chop them into large pieces.

Place the flour on a wooden board and make a well.
You will place the following ingredients into the flour well: beaten eggs, baking soda, sugar, and a pinch of salt.
Mix these ingredients with floured hands until the dough is smooth.
Then, add the almonds.

Place a piece of baking paper on top of a baking sheet.
Butter it and then dust it with flour.
Form the pasta into long fingers on the baking sheet.
Bake the long fingers for 15 minutes and, then, remove them from the oven.
Cut the long fingers into slices about ¼-inch thick.
Place the cut slices on a baking sheet and put them back in the oven for 25 minutes.
When they are a golden brown on one side, turn them over and allow them to become a golden color on the other side.

Summer Picnic

Aperitif: ITALIAN SODA

4 bottles (about 12 ounces each) of assorted flavored syrups
(Use the flavored syrups fro your favorite coffee bars. Choose any flavors that you prefer.)
8 bottles of sparkling water (about 1 quart each)
1 lime sliced
1 lemon sliced
½ cup fresh strawberries
2 fresh peaches sliced
Fresh raspberries
Crushed ice

Fill ten tall glasses with crushed ice.
Add 3 tbsps of flavored syrup to each glass. (Pour it onto the ice already in the glass).
Fill glasses with sparkling water.
Garnish each glass with fresh fruit slices of your choice and serve.

Appetizer: FOCACCIA BREAD

The dough:
2¼ cups tepid water
2 teaspoons active dry yeast
¼ cup olive oil
6½ cups unbleached all purpose flour

These ingredients are to garnish the bread to taste:
olive oil
rosemary
grated cheese
salt

Mix ½ cup water and yeast together in a bowl.
This mixture will start to bubble together-when it does this, you know the yeast is working.
Combine flour and salt together in a large bowl.
Add the yeast mixture, the oil and 1¾ cup of water.
Blend the mixture and, if it is too stiff, add more water a little at a time. You want soft, sticky dough.

Place the dough on a floured board and knead it for about 10 minutes.
Then, place the dough in a greased bowl-cover it and allow it to rise for about 1 to 1½ hours until it doubles in size.
Punch it down with your fists and let it rise a second time.
Divide the dough into three equal pieces and shape each piece into a ball.
Place each ball into an oiled plastic bag and refrigerate for 24 hours.

Remove the dough from the refrigerator about 1½ hours before you are ready to work with it.
Place the dough on a floured board.
Cover it and let it come up to room temperature.
The dough should be doubled in size and should be spongy to the touch.

Heat the oven to 450 degrees F.
Place the dough on flat pans, brush it with olive oil, and sprinkle rosemary and/or grated cheese on top as well as salt to taste. Bake for 15-20 minutes or until golden.
Place the baked foccacia on a rack to cool.

First Course: INSALATA DI RISO (RICE SALAD)

Prepare this recipe at least two hours before eating so that all the flavors have a chance to soak in.

1 cup dried rice
1 can, 6-8 ounces, of tuna (albacore) packed in extra virgin olive oil
1 cup cherry tomatoes
½ pound fresh mozzarella cheese
2 stalks of celery with leaves
½ cup ceci beans (chick peas)
(if dry, soak overnight and then cook until tender; cool the ceci beans before adding them to the salad)
2 tablespoons extra virgin, cold pressed olive oil

Use a good rice, preferably not instant, and cook it according to the instructions on the package.
Drain the rice and let it cool.

Flake the tuna in a small dish.
Cut the mozzarella cheese into small chunks; not too small because fresh mozzarella will break easily.
(Alternately, you can use cilegini mozzarella balls-you don't need to cut these.)

Wash and cut the celery stalks into slices-not too thin-and be sure to pull off any threads from the celery.
Chop celery leaves finely.

Place cooled rice in a large bowl with all the other ingredients, drizzle olive oil on top of the salad,
Gently mix.

Add salt to taste. Save some celery leaves to garnish the top of the salad.

Once the ingredients are mixed, cover and refrigerate them for two hours.

Suggested white wines for dinner:

Chianti
Falenghina

Second Course: FAGIOLINI CON PREZZEMOLO
(FRESH GREEN BEANS WITH PARSLEY)

1 pound fresh string beans
2 tablespoons olive oil
3 fresh cloves of garlic
1/3 cup freshly chopped parsley

Take the tips off the ends of the string beans.
Cook the beans until they are al dente or steam them leaving the tenderness to your liking.
(Do not make them too mushy, or you will lose all the flavor and vitamins.)
Once the beans are cooked, drain them and let them cool to room temperature.

Chop the fresh garlic and parsley.
Place the beans in a small bowl, put in the garlic and parsley, and gently stir.
Drizzle olive oil on top and let the beans stand for about 20 minutes so that the flavors have time to soak in.

This dish can be served cold so you can refrigerate it before you serve it. It also makes great picnic food.

FRESH FRUIT MACEDONIA
Made with fresh fruits in season

BISCOTTI CON LIMONE

5 eggs
1 cup sugar
1 cup sunflower or peanut oil
3 cups flour
3 teaspoons baking powder
rind of 1 whole lemon (grate only the yellow as the white part of the lemon rind is bitter)
1 teaspoon lemon flavoring

Preheat the oven to 350 degrees F. Line 2 cookie sheet pans with parchment paper.

Place all the ingredients in a mixing bowl in the following order:
First beat the eggs with an electric mixer, then beat in the sugar, a little at a time.
Add the oil and then add the flour, a little at a time.
After half of the flour is added, add in the baking powder, grated lemon rind, and lemon flavoring.
Continue to add the remaining flour a little at a time.
Continue beating the dough with an electric mixer.

Place the dough on the parchment paper, on the cookie sheet, in the form of a long log.
Bake the log for 20 minutes. The log should be a golden color.
Remove the log from the oven and cut it into pieces on an angle to form the biscotti.
The thickness of the biscotti should be your preference.
If they are cut thin, they are lower in calories-however, do not cut them so thin that they break apart.

Place the cut biscotti down on parchment paper on a cookie sheet and place them in an oven at 375 degrees F for 10 minutes.
Turn the biscotti over and bake for another 10 minutes. The biscotti should be golden brown.

Please note: Oven temperatures do vary, so be careful not to burn the biscotti.
Also, if you prefer a spongy texture to the biscotti, bake them only once.

LIMONCELLO

In Italy it is you cannot call this drink Limoncello- unless you use the large sweet lemons of Sorrento (which are as sweet as candy and grown without pesticides). There is a trademark on the formula used to make this. However, you can attempt to make something similar here. Try to use fresh if possible organic lemons to get the best quality.

3 organic fresh lemons
2-½ cups pure alcohol for liquors
1 leaf of Melissa
¼ cup sugar
2 cups of spring, distilled or purified drinking water

Wash the lemons, dry and grate the peels, be careful to only take the yellow part of the peel and not the white membrane, which is bitter..
Place in a liquor bottle with alcohol and let sit for 7 days.
Shake bottle every so often.
Heat water, let sugar dissolve in heated water, be careful not to boil.
Remove from heat once sugar is dissolved and let this mixture cool.
Juice 2 lemons.
When syrup has cooled, mix into alcohol mixture with lemon juice.
Let mixture stand for another 7 days.
Filter this mixture and bottle in liquor bottle with cork or top.
Let stand for at least 2 months.
You can store Limoncello in the freezer. Due to its high alcohol content it will not freeze it will only become very cold and add to the refreshing characteristic of this liquor.
This can be used as an after dinner drink or poured over crushed ice for a granite di limoncello.

Una Spaghettata *(a spaghetti party)*

A spaghettata is a A spaghetti party is usually held on Saturday nights at about 12 midnight with friends.

Aperitif: ITALIAN SANGRIA

1 bottle of red wine (preferably Montepulciano or Chianti)
2 cups sparkling water
½ cup Cognac
1 cinnamon stick
2 tbsps sugar
1 orange
1 lemon
2 fresh peaches
4 ounces strawberries
4 ounces raspberries
Orange peel
Cloves
2 tbsps raspberry syrup

Cut fruit and place in large wine carafe with all ingredients except sparkling water.
Let sit for 2 hours, and then add sparkling water and serve.

Appetizer: CROSTINI NAPOLITANI

4 thick slices of bread (crusty Italian type)
2 ounces of fresh mozzarella cheese
2 ounces tomato paste
8 anchovy fillets
olive oil
oregano
salt and pepper to taste

Using an oil can that has a thin spout, pour a light coating of olive oil on each slice of bread
Then equally divide the tomato paste among the 4 slices of bread.
Place 2 anchovy fillets on each slice of bread.
Sprinkle with oregano and then add salt and pepper.

Place baking paper on a baking pan and coat it lightly with oil.
Place each slice of bread on the baking paper
Then bake for about 5 minutes at 400 degrees For until the cheese melts and becomes bubbly.

This recipe serves four people.

First Course: SPAGHETTI WITH SUGO AL POMODORO
GRATED FRESH PARMIGIANO-REGGIANO CHEESE

1 pound fresh plum tomatoes
or 1 16-ounce can plum tomatoes
3 tablespoons olive oil
1 tablespoon onion, chopped finely
2 cloves garlic
Fresh basil leaves
Salt to taste
Freshly grated Parmigiana-reggiano cheese

Place oil in a frying pan and add in onions that have been chopped finely and 2 cloves garlic.
Sauté the onions and garlic until they begin to turn a golden color.
Then add the tomatoes.
Let the sugo cook over low heat, stirring regularly with a wooden spoon.
Add a pinch of salt.
After 20 minutes, most of the liquid should be absorbed and the tomatoes should be concentrated.
Tear, or chop into pieces, two fresh, washed, basil leaves and add them to the tomato sauce.
Stir gently.
Cover the sauce and remove it from the heat.

Place the spaghetti gently into a large pot of rapidly boiling water.
Place the spaghetti in the pan with the sauce and gently toss.
Place servings of spaghetti on individual plates and freshly grate the Parmigiana cheese on to each plate.

Second Course: POLPETTE (MEAT BALLS)

1 pound ground meat made up the following way:
1/3 beef, 1/3 pork, 1/3 veal
¼ cup breadcrumbs (you can add more to make meatballs firm)
2 tablespoons locatelli or parmagiano cheese
2 eggs
Herbs and 1 teaspoon of fresh or dried parsley
Salt to taste (optional)

Mix all the above ingredients.
When they have been mixed well, form the ground meat into meatballs.

Coat a frying pan with about 3-4 teaspoons of olive oil.
You may dip the meatballs into breadcrumbs before frying.
You may also bake the meatballs.

Fry the meatballs, or bake them, until they are brown on the outside.

Dessert: BISCOTTI DI FERRARA

Note: Biscotti means "twice baked" and refers to all cookies that are twice baked, like these are. They may come in all different shapes, but, in America, we are used to seeing these shaped in the typical biscotti shape.

15 egg yolks
2 cups sugar
peel of 1 lemon, grated
1¾ cups flour

Beat the egg yolks with the sugar; add the lemon peel and the flour.
Mix until you achieve a thick dough.
Place the dough on a floured wooden board, lightly dust the dough with flour, and form it into a long log.
Cut the log into small pieces. Form the cut pieces into the shape of an "S."

Butter and flour a piece of baking paper and place the S-shaped pieces, or biscotti, on the baking sheet. When placing the biscotti on top of the baking paper, be sure there is distance between each one.

Bake the biscotti at 320 degrees F for 40 minutes or until golden brown.

After Dinner Drink: ORANGE LIQUEUR (SEE PAGE 134)

APPENDIX 1
WEIGHTS AND MEASURES

COOKING MEASUREMENT EQUIVALENTS

1 tablespoon = 3 teaspoons
1/16 cup = 1 tablespoons
1/8 cup = 2 tablespoons
1/4 cup = 4 tablespoons
1/3 cup = 5 tablespoons + 1 teaspoon
3/8 cup = 6 tablespoons
½ cup = 8 tablespoons
2/3 cup = 10 tablespoons + 2 teaspoons
3/4 cup = 12 tablespoons

1 cup = 48 teaspoons
1 cup = 16 tablespoons

8 fluid ounces = 1 cup
1 pint = 2 cups
1 quart = 2 pints
4 cups = 1 quart
1 gallon = 4 quarts

16 ounces = 1 pound

1 milliliter = 1 cubic centimeter
1 inch = 2.54 centimeters

U.S. TO METRIC CONVERSIONS

1/5 teaspoon = 1 milliliter

1 teaspoon = 5 milliliters

1 tablespoon = 15 milliliters

1 fluid ounce = 30 milliliters

1/5 cup = 47 milliliters

1 cup = 237 milliliters

2 cups = 1 pint = 237 milliliters

4 cups = 1 quart = .95 liters

4 quarts = 1 gallon = 3.8 liters

ITALIAN TERMS USED IN THIS BOOK

A

Agriturismi	(ah-gree-too-rees-mee)	bed-and-breakfasts
Amore	(ah-moh-reh)	love, or, my love
Antipasti	(ahn-tee-pah-stee)	appetizers
Appuntamento	(ah-poon-tah-men-toh	appointment
Arte	(ahr-teh)	art
Autobus	(awoo-toh-boos)	bus

B

Bellezza	(beh-leh-tsah)	beauty, as in, the beauty of ¾
Binario	(bee-nah-ree-oh)	train track
Biscotti	(bees-coh-tee)	cookies
Bis-nonno	(bees-noh-noh)	great grandfather
Braciole	(brah-choh-leh)	steaks or chops
Brodo	(broh-doh)	broth
Bruschetta	(broo-sket-tah)	crusty bread with tomato, etc, on top
Buon'apetito	(boo-ohn ah-peh-tee-toh)	may you have a good meal!

C

Casalinga	(cah-sah-leen-gah)	housewife
Cavaliere	(cah-vah-lee-ere-eh)	knight, or cowboy
Ceci	(cheh-chee)	chick peas
Cena	(cheh-nah)	dinner
Chiesa	(kee-eh-sah)	church
Citta	(chee-tah)	city
Citta d'arte	(chee-tah d-ahr-the)	city of arts
Con	(cohn)	with
Cognate	(coh-neeah-teh)	daughter/sister-in-law
Contorni	(cohn-tor-nee)	side dishes
Cornetti	(core-neh-tee)	croissants or little cones
Crostini	(croh-stee-nee)	croutons or dried bread slices

D

Diavolo	(dee-ah-voh-loh)	devil
Dipende	(dee-pen-deh)	it depends
Doccia	(doh-cha)	shower
Dolce	(dohl-cheh)	sweet, that is, 'it is sweet'
Dolci	(dohl-chee)	sweets

E

| Eccellente | (ech-el-en-teh) | excellent |
| Elettrodomestici | (el-et-roh-dome-es-tee-chee) | electrical appliances for the home |

F

Fagioli	(fah-joh-lee)	beans
Feste	(feh-steh)	feasts, or, holidays
Finocchio	(feen-o-kee-o)	fennel
Forno	(for-noh)	oven or bakery
Fragole	(frah-goh-leh)	strawberries
Frullato	(fruh-lah-toe)	milkshake

G

| Gelato | (je-lah-toh) | ice cream |
| Granita | (grah-nee-tah) | crushed ice with syrup or coffee |

I

Idea	(ee-deh-ah)	idea
Imbottito	(eem-boh-tee-toh)	stuffed
Insalate	(een-sah-lah-the)	salads

L

| Lenticchie | (len-tee-kee-eh) | lentils |
| Limone | (lee-moh-neh) | lemon |

M

Mandorle	(mahn-door-lah)	almond
Mascarpone	(mah-scar-pohn)	a soft, creamy cheese
Mela	(meh-lah)	apple
Mercato	(mehr-kah-toh)	market
Minestra	(mee-neh-strah)	a heavy, filling soup

Mirtilli	(mihr-tih-lee)	blueberries

N

Negozio	(neh-goh-tsee-oh)	store
Noce	(noh-cheh)	nut
Nonna	(noh-nah)	grandmother, grandma
Nonno	(noh-noh)	grandfather, grandpa

O

Otto	(oh-toh)	eight

P

Paese	(pah-eh-seh)	country, or town
Panino	(pah-nee-noh)	bun or sandwich on a bun
Passeggiata	(pah-seh-jah-tah)	walk, as in, going for a walk
Patate	(Pah-tah-teh)	potatoes
Pentolino	(pen-toh-lee-noh)	small, fast train
Pepe	(peh-peh)	pepper, the spice
Pepperone	(peh-peh-roh-neh)	pepper, the vegetable
Per	(pear)	for
Piazza	(pee-ah-tsah)	town square
Piccolo	(pee-coh-loh)	small
Pinoli	(pee-noh-lee)	pine nuts
Polpette	(pol-peh-teh)	meatballs
Pomodoro	(poh-moh-doh-roh)	tomato
Pranzo	(prahn-zhoh)	lunch
Prezzemolo	(preh-tseh-moh-loh)	parsley
Primi	(pree-mee)	the first, as in, first course
Prosciutto	(proh-shoo-toh)	an Italian, cured ham
Prosecco	(proh-seh-koh)	dry sparkling Italian wine

Q

Quanto	(kwan-toh)	how many?

R

Riso	(ree-soh)	rice

S

Salate	(sah-lah-teh)	salted
Sale	(sah-leh)	salt
Salvio	(sahl-vee-oh)	sage
Secondi	(seh-cohn-dee)	the second course
Sfilate	(sfee-lah-tee)	fashion shows
Soffritto	(soh-free-toh)	a lightly sautéed dish
Spiaggia	(spee-ah-jah)	beach
Spumante	(spoo-mon-teh)	sparkling Italian wine
Stracciatella	(strah-chah-tell-ah)	"italian wedding soup"
fragole	(frah-goh-lah)	strawberry
Sugo	(soo-goh)	tomato sauce for pasta
Suocera	(soo-oh-jer-ah)	mother-in-law
Susine	(soo-see-neh)	small plums

T

Tagliatelle	(tah-leeah-tell-eh)	short-cropped pasta noodles
Tartufi	(tar-too-fee)	truffles
Te freddo	(tay fray-doh)	iced tea
Tonno	(toh-noh)	tuna
Torte	(tor-teh)	pies; sometimes, cakes
Treno	(treh-noh)	train

V

Vasoio	(vah-soh-yo)	serving tray
Verde	(vehr-deh)	green
Viaggio	(vee-ah-joh)	voyage, or, journey
Vino	(vee-noh)	wine
Vino	(vee-noh)	wine
Voglio	(voh-ly-lo)	desire
Vongole	(vohn-goh-leh)	mussels

Z

Zia	(dzhee-ah)	aunt
Ziei	(dzee-ay)	uncles
Zio	(dzee-oh)	uncle
Zuppa	(dzoo-pah)	soup

INDEX

Living with cancer?
Come as you are.™

The mission of Gilda's Club New York City is to provide meeting places where men, women and children living with cancer – and their families and friends – can join with others to build emotional and social support as a supplement to medical care. Free of charge and nonprofit, Gilda's Club NYC offers support and networking groups, lectures, workshops and social events in a nonresidential, homelike setting.

Visit us online @ www.gildasclubnyc.org or call 212-647-9700 for information about membership and to make a donation

A portion of book sales goes to Gilda's Club New York City

Sign up for your free online newsletter and receive Maria's tips and ideas on recipes, entertaining, wine pairing, foods, gift giving and more. Go to :
www.marialiberati.com
and sign up now!!

You can also receive Maria's gift-giving and home entertaining tips online in her column for the Sparkling Cards online newsletter at:
http://www.sparklingcards.com

Look for more books in our art of living series:

The Italian Kitchen- coming in late 2006

Festa!! Special Foods and Special Occasions- coming in 2006

The Basic Art of Entertaining- coming in 2007

100 Ways to Cook Pasta- coming in 2007

Pizza, Amore Mio! -coming in late 2006

The Basic Art of Italian Cooking - instructional DVD- coming in 2006

For more info on all upcoming titles go to :

http://www.marialiberati.com

all titles copyright 2006 Art of Living, Prima Media , Inc.
292 Main St, #291
Harleysville, Pa. 19438
publicity@marialiberati.com
primamediapublicity@yahoo.com
1-800-581-9020 x100

Made in the USA